W3C

GH00792442

Dieter Graf

Rhodes
Karpathos
Kos
Southern
Dodecanese

Chálki
Kárpathos
Kássos
Kastellórizo
Kos
Níssiros
Psérimos
Rhodes
Sími
Tílos

Hiking and Swimming for Island-Hoppers
44 Walks on Ten Greek Islands

Graf Editions

Using this illustrated walking guide

AWT stands for Actual Walking Time. This time does not include breaks, wrong turns or sight-seeing. The AWT serves as a personal control as to whether certain route markings, emphasised in **bold print**, have been reached in the given time. These times are an aid for orientation and should not be considered as encouragement to achieve a record performance.

The approximate **overall length** of a walk is specified in hours in the introduction of each tour. These figures do not include time taken for bus trips or extralong breaks. Information concerning the **length of the walks**, the **difference in altitude** and three **levels of difficulty** can also be found there.

Route photos are intended for orientation, for consulting locals and as a stimulus. The corresponding text is marked by ① to ④.

The **route sketches** have been drawn to the best of our knowledge but lay no claim to completeness. We would be grateful for information concerning **changes** in paths and similar data. As a token of our appreciation we will send you a free copy of our next edition. Up-dates can be found in the Internet.

The author Dieter Graf is an architect who has travelled all over the world. He has walked the Aegean Islands since the years when tourism was just beginning there and is considered a connoisseur of the islands.
For this book he spent many months on the Dodecanese Islands.

© 2005 Edition Dieter Graf, Elisabethstr. 29, 80796 Munich, Germany
Tel. 0049-(0)89-271 59 57, Fax 0049-(0)89-271 59 97
www.graf-editions.de

All rights reserved.

Type-Setting: Creativ Mediendesign GmbH, Ottobrunn
Maps: Kurt Zucher, Starnberg
Translation: Nancy Kuehler

Original Title: Wandern auf Griechischen Inseln, Samos, Patmos, Nördlicher Dodekanes (ISBN 3-9808802-0-6)

Cover Photo: Patmos, near Chóra

ISBN 3-9808802-1-4

Contents

Tips for Walks 6
Landscape, Flora, Fauna 10
History 15
Walks 20
Translation Helper F, I, NL, S 27
Island Hopping 158
Helpful Greek Words 159
Explanation of Symbols 160

Kárpathos

Rhodes and the Dodecanese Islands

Connoisseurs of Greece know that "dodéka" means twelve and "níssos" island: the group of twelve islands. A few smaller islands have been added to this group so that meanwhile there are 18 inhabited islands in the "group of twelve". Altogether there are even 163 islands and islets. In this book the ten southern inhabited islands are described.

The Dodecanese Islands are characterised by an enormous variety, not only in respect to landscape but also culturally. The visitor will find wide sandy dunes, small rocky bays, shady pine forests, extinguished volcanoes and the highest mountains in the Aegean. If you are interested, you can view the evidence of a rich cultural history on these old islands on the point of intersection with the orient: ancient temples, medieval fortresses from the crusades, huddled mountain villages and oriental mosques.

The original Greek nature is combined with it all, the friendly people and their hospitality, filoxenía. In Greek "xenos" means "stranger" and "guest" simultaneously. Hospitality was always sacred: Zeus himself watched over this. Perhaps it can't be felt in some of the touristic strongholds on Rhodes any more, but it certainly still can be found off the beaten track, in areas which can only be reached on foot. This book should help you to find the loveliest of the original old mule tracks which will lead you to hidden cloisters and wonderful, isolated spots.

While walking you can discover once again the beauty of slowness and enjoy the variety of the islands with all your senses: the smell of thyme, the clear ringing of the goats' bells, the freshness of clear spring water, the manifold colours of the spring blossoms and especially the friendliness of the people.

Have a good trip!   *Kaló taxídi*!

Walking the Greek Islands

Throughout thousands of years paths and tracks were made for all sorts of very different purposes: for transporting goods from village to village, as pilgrimage paths to the cloisters, to enable farmers to get to the fields. They were lined by walls on both sides and unsuitable for vehicles due to the steep terrain. They spread across the countryside as a thick net.

Our times have torn this net of paths apart by broadening the mule tracks to make them accessible to cars wherever it seemed to be necessary and by pushing aside the characteristic dry walls along the waysides, all financed by money from the EU regional funds. The paths remaining are now superfluous and in ruins and are gradually being forgotten by the inhabitants. This book should help assure that the old mule tracks which still exist, the **monopátia**, are used once again and preserved before definitive deterioration. These are the loveliest walking paths existing. Wherever possible, they are described in this book. Meanwhile, incidentally, there are new funds from the European Union to preserve the remaining net of paths.

The routes described have been walked along again shortly before publication and can be followed without difficulty by people in normal **physical condition**; special firmness of foot is not necessary. The $\checkmark$ markings in the text concern only those who are *very* afraid of heights. Some of the walks are suitable for children. For longer walking tours **short-cuts** are indicated. If you want to walk alone, you should leave information in your hotel in any case.

A few **tips** for wandering: in order to get your blood circulation going, you should begin leisurely for the first fifteen minutes and then continue at the speed that is right for you, where you breathe only through your nose. It is important to eat and especially to drink often, even if you don't feel a need to.

Mule dung on the narrow paths is more certain to lead you further than goat droppings since the goat paths usually end somewhere in the scrub, while mules always return to their stalls.

Steel mesh used as grazing fences can best be climbed over with the help of a pile of stones or at a spot where the "barbs" on top can be turned down most easily. If necessary, wire fences can be opened at the joints and then shut again. Pasture fences are knotted shut on the side where there are two perpendicular rods. You owe it to the farmers whose land you walk across to shut the openings again afterwards, of course. Access to the sea is allowed in Greece as a matter of principle. Due to the good views, the tours normally lead from the mountains to the sea – so take along your swimming gear.

You should absolutely be sure to pick out a nice day for tours in the mountains since there is always the danger of sudden fog formation. Then the few markings aren't much of a help.

On some islands there is an increased risk of forest fires in the summer. For this reason no inflammable objects or pieces of glass should be thrown away along the walk.

No responsibility can be taken for accidents along the walking routes suggested or for possible civil law demands by landowners. Nor can a guarantee be given for bus schedules or opening times. The website-**www.graf-editions.de** can inform you concerning changes along walking routes and similar new information.

Coloured dots and arrows can often be seen as **markings along paths**, but they do not necessarily correspond to the descriptions in this book.

Red-white metal signs with numbers are new and have been put up by domestic organisations. If you have orientation problems, you should always ask the locals about the "monopáti", since you will otherwise be directed to roads for vehicles.

For some of the islands there are road maps from freytag&bernd, Greek Road Editions and recently good Greek maps from the Anavasi publishing house. Other Greek maps are not suitable for walking tours.

Almost all the starting and finishing points are served by public **buses**, even in the low season. In case no buses go on Sundays, **taxis** can be taken. You should absolutely settle the price before you begin the trip. The taximeter is only turned on when you specifically request it. The relatively high price is considered a surcharge for the poor stretches of road. You can arrange a spot with the driver where you will be picked up later or phone for a taxi along the way. This usually works out well. Another possibility for circular walking tours is a relatively reasonable rental car or a rental motor bike. In addition, car drivers also enjoy taking along a wanderer who waves him down.

Despite efforts, **environmental protection** still remains an unsolved problem, so some things you see lying around while walking through the countryside will not always correspond to your sense of order and environmental stipulations. The Greek remains true to his character: he is also very generous with his garbage.

Sufficient **wandering gear** includes a backpack for a day, shoes with good soles (no sandals), comfortable socks, long trousers or zipper trousers*, a mobile phone possibly, binoculars, a whistle, a small flashlight and picnic equipment with a salt-shaker. In the spring and fall, rain gear is a necessity. A compass would also be good but is not necessary if you have a somewhat good sense of orientation.

*The legs of zipper trousers which also have vertical zippers can be zipped together to form a pad to sit on at the beach. And if you connect both zippers, you have a chic skirt for visiting monasteries.

Climate and Walking Season

The typical, temperate Mediterranean climate with a hot summer and mild, rainy winter predominates on the Dodecanese. The maximum **air temperature** is 32 °C in August (at night 22 °C). In the winter the temperature sinks to 15 °C (7 °C) in February. Snow can fall every 3–4 years in the mountains over 1000 m high and lie there for a short while.

The **water temperatures** are lowest in February at 16 °C and reach an almost subtropical 25 °C in August. You can go swimming from the end of May at 19 °C through October (22 °C).

The mountains in Asia Minor help the islands located before them to get more rain than is found in the more western Cyclades. However, the rainy days are strewn irregularly throughout the year. Most of the rain falls in December and January, when it rains on about 14 days. You must still calculate with 3 days of rain in May, while there is absolute dryness from June to August. Statistically October has 6 days of rain again, but it is not very plentiful.

The number of **hours of sun** per day corresponds to this. In December and January the very strong winter sun shines only about 4.5 hours. Even in May the wanderer must reconcile himself to 10.1 hours of sun daily and the swimmer in August to 12.1. October is pleasant for autumn walkers once again, with 7.8 hours of sun per day.

Strong **north winds** are characteristic of the Aegean Islands, with three to four Beaufort on a yearly average. One reason for this is the air pressure difference between the Azore highs and the hot low pressure areas above the Persian Gulf. In the transition season, especially in April and May and then October and November, the Boréas dominates, a cool, wet north wind. In the summer, mainly between May and September, the famous etesien winds, called the meltémia (from the Turkish word "meltem") often blow for days under a cloudless blue sky, regularly strong from north to northeast, with velocities of five to six Beaufort. The sky can then be somewhat overcast. Towards evening the meltémi usually slackens somewhat, but it can also blow with quite great strength for days on end.

The schirókko occurs less frequently, but especially in the spring. It comes from the hot Sahara desert, picks up moisture over the Mediterranean to bring the Aegean warm humidity from the south.

On the Greek islands there are several different **seasons for walking tours**. Anyone wanting to give his eyes a treat should plan his tour around Easter. It might be somewhat cool and even muddy, but the countryside is grass-green, poppy-red and broom-yellow; the houses and alleyways are freshly white-washed. Even just the preparations for the Greek Easter celebration are worth the trip. However, you can't go swimming yet, and some hotels and tavernas are still closed. In April it can rain at the spur of a moment. The Greeks divide the year in three parts, and this one is called "the time blossoming and maturing".

In May and June the blossom time is already partially over, but, since it is very warm and the number of tourists is still limited, this is probably the loveliest time for walking. Beginning at the end of May the water has a pleasant temperature.

The main tourist season in July and August is not highly recommended for walking tours due to the heat. It is the "dry period" in Greece. The north winds, which blow consistently, still make the temperatures bearable, but at noon a shady spot under a tree is advisable. Harvest time begins in July. On August 15, the Assumption of the Virgin, in the eastern church called "Passing Away Peacefully", there are great celebrations everywhere with roast lamb, music and dance.

From the beginning of September on, the heat is over and the sea still has a pleasant temperature for swimming until the end of October. Now longer walking tours can be taken once again, but only until about 6 p.m. due to the shorter period of daylight. The land has become yellow and brown, the fields bear their fruit, and everywhere you meet friendly farmers harvesting their last crops. Starting at the beginning of October it can start to rain again. The restaurants and hotels gradually shut down, and some owners travel to their winter residences in Athens. Others put on camouflage suits, reach for their guns and search through the brush. A million Greeks are passionate hunters. In November there is usually a change in climate, with heavy rainfall. Then it becomes unpleasant. The period from November to February is called the "rain season". Although there are some warm, sunny days around Christmas, it is more pleasant at home.

Geology

Two different types of geological origin have been established. The **northern Dodecanese islands** are shelf islands. They rise 100 to 200 metres out of the submarine Asiatic continental base, the shelf, and were separated from the Asian continent as the geological history of the earth developed. The northern Aegean was not flooded by the sea until after the last ice age. After various actions of rising and falling, the islands took on their present form. Several volcanoes have broken through the shelf, as on Níssiros or Kos. The floor of the sea falls down to 1000 m towards the west and forms the geological border to Europe.

On the other hand, Rhodes and Kárpathos together with Crete form a broad arc of islands extending from Asia Minor to the Peloponnes. These islands rise up from underwater calcareous (chalky) mountains which fall off sideways to a level of 2500 metres under the water. They originated 50 million years ago through the pressure exerted by the African continental plate onto the European. The highest mountains in the Aegean rise up along this backbone of islands: the Atáviros on Rhodes (1215 m), the Kalilímni on Kárpathos (1214 m) and the Ida, which towers 2456 m above Crete.

Fauna

Larger wild animals are not present - due to the mostly small-sized vegetation. It is only on Rhodes that there have been roe deer since antique times; these were bred again by the Italians. Along the way you often come upon the small common lizard, which can be up to 10 cm long. The dragon-like agama (hardun) ① is its bigger relative and is up to 30 cm long. It disappears immediately at the slightest approach.

The careful wanderer will rarely see snakes. There is only one poisonous type: the horn or sand viper (vipera ammodytes meridionalis) ②. It can be up to 50 cm long and as thick as two thumbs. A healthy adult hardly need fear a deadly bite.

The non-poisonous sand-boa is about the same size; it lives in

very concealed spots. The non-poisonous four-striped-adder reaches an adult length of more than a metre and a width almost as thick as an arm. Its size is frightening, but it is harmless, as is its much smaller relative, the ring-snake.

Scorpions, reaching a size of up to 5 cm, also live here. A bite is rather painful but not deadly. They love to hide in shoes.

Land turtles ③ have become rare.

You can discover crabs, frogs and eels along the rivers which carry water all year round.

You will meet goats and sheep most frequently along the walks. They are shy and run away frightened when surprised. The breeding of goats is subventioned, and their gnawing has led to great damage.

Flora

Along with Spain, Greece has the greatest variety of plants in Europe. Nevertheless, since antique times forests on the Aegean islands have been cut down for building ships or have become

victims of the forest fires in summer, causing some parts of the landscape to seem like barren chalk formations. The islands of the Dodecanese are, however, mainly green and fruitful since the clouds collect in the mountains of Asia Minor and bring greater amounts of rain in winter.

The stock of trees consists mainly of extensive forests of aleppo pines ①. The resin for retsina wine is won from these. Taller evergreen oaks and kermes oaks ② grow in protected regions which are rich in water. Unassuming, salt-tolerant tamarisks ③ are found along beaches. Plane-trees ④ shade the village squares and slender cypresses the cemeteries. Acacias, poplars, alders, maples and eucalyptus trees ⑤ can also be found, as well as mulberry trees ⑥ and carobs ⑦. Among the fruit trees there are pomegranates, fig trees ⑧ and citrus fruits. The olive tree, which looks strangely deformed as it gets older, is the most characteristic tree in the landscape.

On slopes and mountain-tops, dry shrubs reaching a height of up to half a metre predominate, thorny brush called "phrýgana" in Greek. Broom, thorny knap-weed (centauria spinosa), heat-

her, spiny spurge plants (euphorbia) ⑨ ⑩ are their typical representatives, often shaped like hedgehogs.

Thicker bush or tree groups up to two metres high with evergreens and bushes with hard leaves are not found as frequently. This "high macchia" is called "xerovumi" in Greek. Kermes oaks with serrated leaves ② , juniper and mastic bushes ⑪ are particularly predominant. Mastic bushes are used for manufacturing rubber and raki spirits.

Too much goat grazing has caused the beginnings of larger vegetation to be kept low. Sometimes burnt areas can be seen. The reason behind this planned burning is for goats to have the freshly growing sprouts as food. In the short term this goal is achieved, but inedible plants such as Jerusalem sage, squill or asphodel ⑫ grow here quickly.

Agaves (agave americana) ⑬ often line the lanes and paths. This thorny leaf plant has only grown in the Mediterranean area since the 16th century. Fig-cactus ⑭, with its thorny but tasty fruit, is also wide-spread.

A surprisingly abundant splendour of flowers appears in the

spring. Even in January there are anemones and crocus blossoms. From February to April white and red blossoming rock-roses ⑮, iris, yellow daffodils, hyacinths, lupines, chrysanthemums and broom add magic to the landscape with their cheery colours, and the poppy adds its bright red.

The smaller orchids are an adornment of spring, if only for a short time. The bee orchid ⑯, lax-flowered orchid, tongue orchid (serapia) and dragon arum ⑰ can be seen frequently.

In May and June the main blossoming season comes to an end, but summer doesn't mean brown desert by any means. Bougainvillea ⑱ radiates its bright colours on the house walls, and blossoming plants can still be found in protected moist spots, especially the red-blooming oleander bushes. Hardy gold thistles still bloom along the paths ⑲.

In the late summer and fall, the flora begins to come alive again and blossom after the first brief rain showers. Meadow-saffron, heather and squill reveal themselves along with the crocus-like stellaria bergia, dandelions, thistles and cyclamen (sowbread).

Many of the plants contain ethereal oils. In the heat of the day you can especially appreciate the pleasantly spicy aroma of thyme, rosemary, lavender, oregano, camomile and fennel. Sage ⊠, capers ⊠ and other kitchen spices often border the walking paths on the islands.

Historical Data

The first traces of mankind on Rhodes date back to around 5000 BC and are found in caves. The islands' position between Europe and Asia soon makes them a bridge between the two cultures and one of the oldest landscapes in Europe to be cultivated by man from a very early age. The first immigrants, the Carians, come from Asia Minor around 2800 BC. Four thousand years ago the Phoenicians come and give the Occident the concepts of writing and money.

After the downfall of Crete's palaces around 1400 BC, Minoan settlers land and give the impulse for the first blossoming of culture here. Around 1200 BC these settlements are, however, relinquished. Starting in 1500 BC, the Achaeans immigrate from the Peloponnes. After 1100 BC the Aegean islands and Asia Minor are colonised in several waves by peoples from Greece. The Ionians dominate on Sámos; south of this the Spartan Dorians prevail. Here the Rhodian city of Líndos soon attains outstanding importance. From Rhodes, colonies as far as in Sicily and Spain are founded. In the 8th century the "Hexapolis" is formed, a league of three of Rhodes' city-states with Kos as well as Knidos and Halikarnass in Asia Minor. Délos becomes the intellectual and cultural centre of the Athenian-Delian League. This protective alliance against Persia binds the Greeks of the Aegean and Asia Minor with Athens. Starting in 540 BC, the Persian Empire has extended its influence to the coast of Asia Minor. The Persian Wars begin in 490 BC.

The Classical Period   (490–336 BC) The Dorian islands fight on the side of the enemy at the beginning of the Persian Wars, but they, too, are on Athens' side for the final triumph over the Persians in 449 BC. Immense riches are amassed on Délos during the Golden Age which follows. When Athens carries off the treasure and tries to make vassals of its allies, the islands fight against Athens in allegiance with Sparta in the Peloponnesian War. The outcome is a forever weakened Greece. Athens loses all its importance, but the newly founded city of Rhodes, with

80,000 inhabitants, is soon one of the richest cities in the world at that time.

Hellenistic Period   (338–146 BC) The Macedonians in northern Greece take over the Greek culture after conquering Greece in 338 BC and then shortly afterwards the islands. For a short period Alexander the Great, a Macedonian, takes this culture, henceforth known as "Hellenism", as far as India. Under his successors Rhodes strengthens its power. Sculptures from Rhodes attain a world-wide reputation; the Colossus of Rhodes, 30 m high, is created. Along with Alexandria, Rhodes is the most important city in the Mediterranean.

Roman Period   (146 BC – 330 AD) After 146 BC the Romans, as the next rulers, also make the Greek culture their own, thus helping its spread throughout Europe. The Greek culture becomes that of the Occident. Important Romans visit the Dodecanese, either as visitors at the health resorts of the Asklipieion on Kos or as scholars at the school of rhetoric on Rhodes, among them Caesar, Cicero, Cassius, Cato, Brutus, Tiberius and Pompey. In 51 AD the apostle Paul travels through the islands, which have very early contact to Christianity, later the state religion in Eastern Roman Empire (Byzantine Empire) in 391 AD. When Délos becomes a free port, the economic importance of Rhodes comes to an end.

The Byzantine Period   (330–127 AD) While the Western Roman Empire is declining during the migration of peoples in 476 AD, the eastern part of the Imperium Romanum remains an upholder of Graeco-Roman culture. Byzantium, the second Rome, turns eastwards, brings Christianity to the Slavs and spreads Greek ideas as far as Moscow, which later becomes known as the Second Byzantium or Third Rome. The new Islamic ideas also influence Greece in the 8th and 9th centuries. In the feud over pictures, iconoclasm, the admissibility of a pictorial representation of God and the Saints, is disputed.

Europe begins to drift apart in cultural terms; the religious differences also deepen. It is disputed whether the Holy Ghost only emanates from God the Father or also from his Son, as the Roman Catholic Church believes. Another controversy is the corporal ascension of Mary, which is considered as a "peaceful passing away" in the Orthodox Church. In 1054 the schism or final separation of the Eastern Greek-Orthodox Church from the Western Latin Church of Rome comes about.

In these uncertain times the Aegean Islands are often attacked and occupied by the Vandals, Goths, Normans and then the Saracens. The inhabitants of the islands withdraw into the mountain villages. It isn't until the 9th century that Byzantium can consolidate its power once again. Now, however, in the wake of the Persians, Avars, Arabs and Seljuks, a new great Asian power has assembled on the eastern borders of Byzantium: the Turkish Ottoman Empire. It pushes westward with immense force. In 1095 the Eastern Roman Empire requests help from Pope Urban II, and the crusades begin. They are a fiasco. Jerusalem, which has been a place of pilgrimage until now, cannot be held on to by the Christians. (see also p. 57) During the fourth crusade, one of the most short-sighted campaigns in history is initiated. Due to trade rivalries, Venice induces the crusaders to plunder the Byzantine capital, Constantinople, in 1204. The quadriga on San Marco square is one part of the loot. Byzantium is too weak to ever recover again and is conquered by the Turks in 1453.

The Era of the Knights   (1204–1523) For most of the islands, Venetian and Genuan domination begins after the spoilage of Constantinople. Later some of them are sold to the orders of knighthood driven out of Jerusalem or are snatched by them from Byzantium, the nominal owner, as in the case of Rhodes. From these sites the orders of the knighthood want to protect Christianity, even if it means piracy. The orders have only a short time on the Greek islands. After capturing Constantinople, the Great Ottoman Empire directs all its energy towards conquering Europe. After the fall of Rhodes, the strongest fortress of Christianity, in 1523, the Turks push on further to Vienna and Malta. Here their power weakens.

The Turkish Era   (1523–1912) The Fall of Constantinople in 1453 marks the end of the thousand-year-old advanced Greek civilisation. Learned Byzantine fugitives bring the Greek way of thinking back to the West once again, paving the way for the Renaissance. From this time on, the fortune of the Orthodox Church is determined in Moscow, which also assumes the Byzantine double-headed eagle and the Roman Imperial claim for power.

Yet the whole of Greek life, from music to diet, is dominated by Turkish influence for the next 350 years. This influence is still recognisable to a degree today. There is somewhat greater freedom on the islands, but this always depends on the current representative of the "Sublime Porte" in Istanbul. The Orthodox Church proves to be the safeguard of Greek culture. Children are taught the Greek language and writing in secret schools.

Independent Greece   (since 1821) Finally, at the beginning of the 19th century, Europe reflects on its cultural roots. The political stability of post-Napoleonic Europe and Classicism in art increase awareness of eastern Europe. Philhellenists from many countries support the Greek struggle for independence after 1821, the Great Powers in Europe help diplomatically, and Greece becomes a part of Europe again.

However, not the islands in front of the Turkish coast. The London Protocol of 1830 regulates the new order in the Aegean area and determines their continued dependence on Turkey. There is only greater autonomy in administration.

The Italian Dodecanese   (1912–1947) Italy, which has come too late for dividing up this part of the world, begins a successful war against Turkey in North Africa in 1912 and helps itself to a part of the "sick man on the Bosporus". Following this there is a Greek uprising on the Dodecanese. The Turks leave the islands, and the Italians appear here as the new masters. The Dodecanese are later integrated into Mussolini's new Imperium Romanum as "Italian possessions in the Aegean". After his end, German troops occupy them from 1943 until the end of the war. "Ennosis", the late return to the fatherland, finally takes place in 1947, after a brief period of British administration.

After World War II   With Western help during the civil war from 1945 to 1949, Greece avoids the fate of the other Balkan countries, and doesn't disappear behind the Iron Curtain. Gradually Greece is accepted in the most important European institutions. European subventions lead to an improvement in the infrastructure and help tourism to develop. This becomes the most important economic sector in the country. After the economic recovery, the drachma, the oldest currency in the world, is replaced by the euro in 2002.

Sími

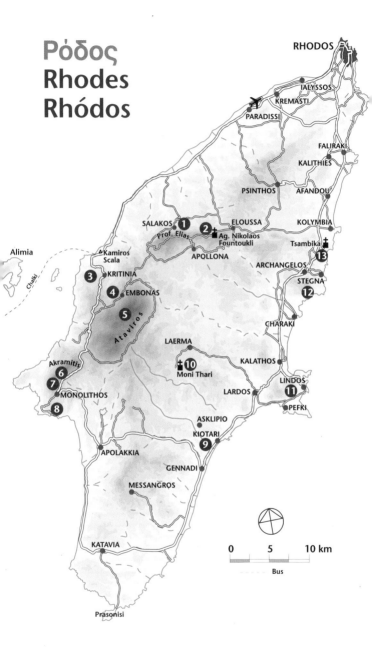

Ρόδος
Rhodes
Rhódos

RHODOS

IALYSSOS
KREMASTI
PARADISSI

FALIRAKI
KALITHIES

PSINTHOS   AFANDOU

Alimia

SALAKOS **1** **2** ✝ ELOUSSA   KOLYMBIA
Prof. Elias. Ag. Nikolaos
Fountoukli   Tsambika **13**
▲Kamiros   APOLLONA
Scala
3 KRITINIA   ARCHANGELOS
4 EMBONAS   STEGNA
5   **12**
Atáviros
                   CHARAKI
LAERMA
                   KALATHOS
Akramitis **6**   ✝ **10**
7   Moni Thari   LINDOS
MONOLITHOS   LARDOS   **11**
8   PEFKI
                   ASKLIPIO
                   KIOTARI
APOLAKKIA   **9**

GENNADI

MESSANGROS

                   0   5   10 km
KATAVIA   Bus

Prasonisi

Even in Roman times there was active tourism on these age-old islands, pampered by the sun and brimming with culture. Refined Roman families sent their sons to the rhetoric school of Poseidonios on the "Rose Island".

Today Rhodes, with over a million visitors, is the most touristic island in the Aegean apart from Crete. This tourism, however, is concentrated on the beaches in the north.

After visiting the picturesque medieval old town, a world culture heritage site, the connoisseur of nature and landscape quickly moves on to the middle of the island.

Tourism hasn't established itself everywhere here yet. You can wander through pristine woods and mountains and discover chapels with important frescoes here and there. Yet there is no need to give up beaches.

Due to its great supplies of water, the island is green and fruitful. A relief map of the island shows a mountainous spine parallel to the coast in the western part. It is dominated by the 1215 metre-high Atáviros, the highest mountain in the Dodecanese. To the east and south of it, wooded hillsides spread out. Far to the south the landscape becomes flat and less spectacular. Here scrub dominates the vegetation.

A rental car is the easiest means of getting to various walks. Buses only are of help to the wanderer on the east side of the island, where Lindos, a lovely but crowded town at night, is a good base for walkers.

In the western part it is best to spend the night in the unspoilt mountain villages. There are only bus connections to here in the afternoon.

Good road maps can be purchased from ReiseKnowHow, tc travel maps, Freytag&Berndt, Road Editions and, beginning in 2004, from Anavasi, with data for walkers.

Starting out from Rhodes you can also take walking excursions to the neighbouring islands, Chálki and Sími.

❶ Alpine Chalets on Mount Elias

This four-hour mountain walk leads from Salákos about 500 m steeply but wonderfully uphill past two abandoned inns from the time of the former Italian administration and to the peak of Profitis Elias. Salákos has good bus connections. It is, however, worth thinking about spending the night there and enjoying the delightful atmosphere of dinner next to the babbling fountain. The local colour makes you forget that you are on a touristic island.

AWT 0.00	At the **village square in Salákos** go along the slightly rising street to a right curve with a little bus stop and turn left at the sign "footpath" onto a cement road. After walking along it for 100 m, turn up to the right uphill onto a
0.05	**tractor track** (sign). *In front of a wayside shrine* turn left and, in spring, walk upwards through a rich green landscape. The zigzag path is slightly shaded by kermes oaks and offers the wanderer a splendour of blossoms – peonies, violets and even orchids ①. Despite the many dashes of colour from the flowers, remember to pay attention to the dotted red path markings. Once you have the steep
0.35 ★	part of the **ascent behind you**, you will see some antennas and walk on a flat level through a pine forest. In an opening up to the right between the trees the St. Michael Chapel can be seen. The detour of a few metres to get there is worth it because it is a lovely spot for a picnic. Otherwise, continue on to the wide path, where you turn to the left immediately onto a marked footpath. This leads to two dilapidated houses (left) and from there to
0.50	the right on up to the two **hotels** ②.

> *These inns, named after the heraldic animals of Rhodes, the stag and the hind (elafas and elafína), were built in 1926 during the time of the Italian administration. The governor of the Dodecanese, the "Italian possessions in the Aegean", spent the hot season here, when the heat was too oppressive down in the town. After the war they were used as hotels, but the constructions have been slumbering like Sleeping Beauty property since 1990, waiting for an investor's kiss.*
>
> *On the other side of the street a rustical café greets exhausted walkers and loud Jeep drivers.*

50 m to the right of the café a path with steps leads upwards, on past the deserted governor's residence (left) to
the formerly Catholic chapel. Behind this several footpaths lead through the wildly romantic mountain land-
1.05   scape on up to the **peak**, where it is easy for anyone to
find the right stone to sit down on to rest. The peak with
the antennas on the opposite side belongs to the military;
Apollónas spreads out in the high plateau below. By good
visibility the Italian governor probably came up here, too,
and convinced himself with his binoculars that his islands were still all there.

To descend, choose a path towards the antennas which
1.25   first leads in the direction of the next peak, then downhill
and in front of the approach road to the antennas left
again to the **hotels**.

> *Alternative:* The path described below is known only to
> a few locals. Although a short section of it is filled up
> and it is barely recognisable in some places, there are
> coloured markings along it. You must climb over
> harmless rocks a couple of times, but there is no pro-
> blem with the general orientation.
>
> If you want to avoid this, return down on the same
> path you followed to come up.

1.25   Directly in front of the **hotels** a dirt road leads downhill
between the ruins of the small squad's quarters to the
1.30   abandoned **power supply buildings**. Don't worry: you
haven't been able to get electric shocks here for a long
time.

Beneath these there is a spring called *Perivoli*. A monopáti
begins at the well house and leads downhill on the left of
the metal water pipes. At first the path is clearly recognis-

1.35 able but gets lost near a little moss-covered **stone house**. From here on you continue without a path, first somewhat to the left; then you approach the stream bed again and go left about 30 to 40 m parallel above it. The water pipe is also on the right. Before a field of rubble you **cross**
1.45 **over the stream bed** and later find the old path leading downwards again. As an alternative, you can go down directly next to the water pipe. In a flatter section after a clearing you will find a path to the left leading through a
2.00 small forest of kermes oaks. Then **you can see the houses** of Salákos. The path ends in front of a mesh fence designed to keep out wild goats. If you go 10 m to the right of this, cross over the water pipe, open and shut the wires of the fence, then you reach the tractor track you used on the way up. Walk along to the right, on past the wayside
2.15 shrine and then to the left to the main street in **Salákos**.

▶ The dreamlike **hotel** "Nymfi" (Tel 224 60-222 06 and 22346) has only four rooms. It is in an old, somewhat antiquated Italian villa in the style of its era.

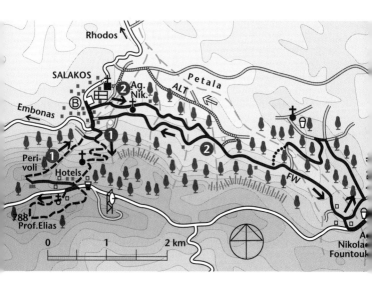

❷ A Wealth of Pictures in Fountoúkli

The chapel Ayios Nikoláos Fountoúkli is one of the main cultural sights on Rhodes. This five-hour walking tour leads you there from Salákos, along paths which are easy to find and through a shady forest as well as old olive groves. The hilly terrain can, however, be strenuous. Along the way there is a fountain, but there are no tavernas.
See map on previous page.

AWT
0.00   Starting at the tranquil **Platía in Salákos**, walk up the main street for about 200 m until you reach a lovely fountain (right) and then continue downhill along a wide cement path across from the fountain. Passing the cemetery

0.05   (with an interesting church!) and a **cement wall** on the left, you come to the shady valley ①. Jump over two streams here, and then, as the path continues uphill, you can see the islands of Chálki and Alímia to the left. At the top of the hill, turn off to the right and then later at the

0.15   water meter to the left, to get to the (first) **Nicholas Chapel**. From here you go on downhill to the left to reach the upper edge of the fields on the Pétala plains.

After a house (left) you pass by a gate made of chicken wire, pass giant pines, cross over a water ditch and reach a

0.30   wide **glade with olive trees** (left). After another water
0.35   ditch, you walk uphill to a wide **sandy track** and continue to the left there. This sandy track gets broader from year to year. It also serves as a fire-corridor, but parts of it are ploughed up without any consideration for nature.

At a fork continue uphill to the right along the wide track and pass by a broad grove of olive trees. At the end of the

0.55   grove there are **goat stalls**. After this, the way continues on downhill. The driver of the bulldozer seems to have lost control over his vehicle completely here. He flattened

1.10   everything to a breadth of 30 metres. At the **turn-off** to the left down into the valley, go on **straight** towards the antenna on the mountain. After a sparse olive garden you come to the ruins of a house, then to the street, where

1.35   you go left to the **chapel Ayios Nikoláos Fountoúkli** ②. *This cruciform-domed church has four apses and was established around 1500 by a high official in memory of his three children who had died of the plague. The family is re-*

presented at eye level in the apse across from the altar: the parents with the model of the church, the children praying in the Garden of Eden. Christ is blessing them. Next to him are his mother and John the Baptist.

All the walls are completely covered with frescoes. Among them, Christ's baptism, Lazarus rising from the dead and the escape to Egypt are pictured. 25 saints looking down from the dome regard the tired wanderer with pity.

There used to be a cloister on the terrace area; today it is a picnic spot with a fountain and fire station.

You return to the olive grove on the same path at first, but

1.40
1.45 at the **second site of ruins** you take the dirt path downhill to the right and later at the **turn-off** you go uphill to the left. After the ascent you can see the sea on both sides and the village of Dimyla to the right. Salákos, your goal is still quite far away!

First you walk on flat terrain along the crest, then steeply

2.00 downhill to where the **paths cross**. Here you walk downhill to the left and one minute later turn off sharply to the left! Narcotic scents from the pines accompany you on

2.10 your way down to the **valley floor**, where frogs bustle about in the water holes. The wide path through the woods crosses the stream bed in a sharp left curve. Right at this spot, follow the course of the stream to the right without a path for a short while, then go uphill to the left

2.15 to return to the wide **sandy track** from the way there.

Now you continue uphill to the right, past the goat stalls and down to the narrower turn-off to the right.

> **Alternative:** By going to the right, you can also reach Salákos if you keep to the left at all the forks. This stretch leads back uphill behind the **Pétala valley** and

takes 15 minutes longer. The way described below along the wide track, however, offers lovelier views.

If you stay on the wide sandy track, the turn-off to the right which you came by on the way here (= AWT 0.35) will soon appear. You should go downhill to the left here,

3.00 past a typical Greek **sheep pen** (left) and then past the Nicholas Chapel again (right) to the strangely ludicrous area for festivals. At the water basin, a dirt path leads

3.20 down to the right to the hotel "Nymfi" in **Salákos**.

Translation of special words

English	Français	Italiano	Nederlands	Svenska
boulder	bloc de rocher	masso	Rotsblok	klippblock
cairn	marquage	segnalato di pietre	Markeringssteen	vägmärke
dirt road	chemin rural	sentiero di camp.	Onverharde weg	åkerväg
ditch	fossé	fosso	Sloot	sänka
fork	bifurcation	bifurcazione	Wegsplitsing	vägskäl
gap	brèche	breccia	Bres	inskärning
glade	clairière	radura	Open plek in bos	glänta
gorge	gorge	abisso	Kloof	ravin
gravel	pierraille	ghiaia	Steengruis	stenskärvor
grove	bosquet	bosco	Bosschage	lund
gully	cours d'eau	letto di fiume	Waterloop	vattendrag
heath	lande	brughiera	Heide	hed
hollow	dépression	depressione	Glooiing	sänka
incline	pente	pendio	Helling	sluttning
past	près de	accanto a	naast	jämte
pebble	caillou	ciottolo	Kiezel	grus
pen	bergerie	stalla ovile	Stal	stall
ravine	ravin	abisso	Ravijn	ravin
rim	bords	orlo	Rand	kant
ridge	crête	cresta	Bergkam	bergskam
rubble	éboulis	ditriti	Steengruis	stenar
saddle	crête	sella	Bergrug	bergsrygg
scrub	fourré	sterpaglia	Doornbos	snår
slope	pente	pendio	Helling	sluttning
stream bed	lit	letto di fiume	Waterloop	vattendrag
strenuous	fatigant	faticoso	inspannend	ansträngande
trail	sentier	sentiero	Pad	stig
turn-off	bifurcation	biforcazione	Afslag	avtagsväg
well	puits	pozzo	Bron	brunn

❸ The Citadel on the Sea

On this easy-to-find four-hour circular walking tour, you pass through a fertile valley, rest at a shady village square, go for a swim in the sea and experience the sunset from the lovely vantage point of the ruins of a crusade citadel.
A shorter two-and-a-half-hour tour leaves out the ascent to the village of Kritiniá.

AWT   The walk begins beneath the citadel of Kritinía. If you come by **bus**, you must calculate an additional 25 minutes from Kámiros-Skala on the street to get there as well as 25 more minutes to return.

0.00   From the **lower parking lot** (with snack area) of the **Kastélos Kritiniá** go back down the approach road and turn right onto a narrow dirt road after a few steps. The citadel, which is situated above you to the right, can be saved for viewing the sunset. At the end

0.07   of the road, turn left onto a wider **dirt road** and head straight on through a hollow with fields and arable land. You can soon see the goal up in the hills, the village of Kritiniá, and above it the 1215 m-high Atáviros, the highest mountain on Rhodes.

0.15   The dirt road makes a **curve to the left** ①, and here you turn to the right onto a 5 m-wide strip similar to a cultivated field. At the end of the "field", you can see a foot path leading downwards and accompanied by winding irrigation hoses. At the bottom it meets a

0.20   **sandy road**, which you follow uphill to the left.

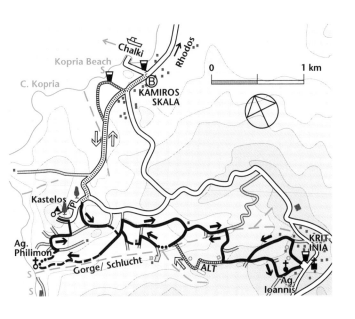

      Short Cut: Later you will return to this place (= AWT
      1.40). This is where you could now turn down to the
      right to the potato field and thus take the "small tour".
Turn left at the first fork, then right at the following one,
before you walk along the foot of the slope rising to the
left. Tomatoes, potatoes and many other vegetables are
0.25 planted on this plain. At the fork, turn left. A **farmhouse** is
above the path, surrounded by glorious chaos. At the next
fork, keep to the left. To the right you are approaching the
reedy stream bed, which you will cross over on a cement
0.30 pipe at the next **fork** to the right.
While you work your way steeply uphill, you have a wonderful view of the citadel and Chálki behind it.
Pay no regard to the turn to the left, and you will come to
0.40 a **water basin** (right). Continue on to the left. When the
paths cross near a boulder (right), continue straight on.
The path then continues in a wide arc to the right until it
meets up with another path. Turn left here onto the path
dug into the ground and leading uphill until you reach a
chapel.

*The **chapel Ayios Ioánnis Pródromos** is located like a jewel, set between two cypress trees. Over the years the flagstone roof has become covered with a thick layer of paint. Inside there are impressive frescoes from the time it was built, in the 13th or 14th century. Salome's Dance before Herod and the Beheading of John the Baptist are outstanding.*

1.00 Following a cement path, you soon arrive at the shady village square, the piatsa of **Kritiniá**, for a well-earned rest. After looking around this village, which was founded by the Cretans, and also having seen the remarkable church, walk down the cement path along the left side of the piatsa facing the valley. Pass the water basin (left) and continue straight on towards the valley in a wide arc to the left. At times the path is almost flat and leads between the terraced fields, ending back at the crossing of the paths near the boulder, where you now wander on downhill the

1.15 right to the **water basin**.

> *Alternative:* If you turn left here, in a few minutes you will come to an oblong water basin from which a very old, round **grain mill** is operated. From here, however, you must return to the valley without a path.

The path leads away from the water basin back down to the valley and turns to the left at the reeds. At the "chaos farmer's" walk down to the left this time. When the dirt path ends, continue to the right across a field to another dirt path and follow it through green gardens and fields until it forks at a fence. Turn left and you will come to a

1.30 **tool storage area**. Turn to the right after this at a small house. At the end of the dirt path, a footpath connects to another dirt path, which you should follow to the right.

At the fork, turn to the left and you will arrive back at the
1.40 spot where you **came downhill** earlier (= ATW 0.20).
This time you go downhill to the left into an intensively
used fertile valley. The path ends to the right of a potato
field. Of course, you will discover the continuation of the
1.45 **path** [2] immediately, as it leads on up to the right now. It
meanders wonderfully above a rugged gorge and through
all the spices belonging to the Greek cuisine: thyme, sage,
1.55 marjoram and many more. It ends at the **sea** in a flat
coastal area where the ruins of the early Christian Phili-
mon basilica [3] have been exposed. If you want to take a
swim, there is a beach with fine sand further to the south.
Directly above the excavations a steep path marked by
cairns leads to flat land from which you walk on further
2.05 towards the castle. Walk to the left on the **road**, leaving
out four or five left turns, continuing on beneath the castle [4], which presents itself from its wildly romantic side
here. After passing it on the side, turn left, continue
uphill along a road and you will arrive at a street on the
2.15 left leading to the **castle**.

*The **Kastélos Kritiniá** is the best preserved castle of the order of Saint John on Rhodes. The castle-keep, St. George's chapel and the shield wall are in good condition. The coats of arms of the Grand Masters of the Order, who had the castle constructed beginning in 1472, are set in the outer walls. The view across the sea to Chálki is especially enchanting towards evening.*

If you must return **to Kámiros-Skala** on foot, take the way down to the parking area (along a small forest path) and then along the street further downhill to the left. Perhaps you will still have the time and energy for a little visit to Johnny's lovely fish taverna above Kopriá Beach. It is, of course, also recommended to the drivers as well.

▶ In Kámiros-Skala you can **spend the night** in the *Pension Linos*, Tel. 224 40-312 64.

❹ Grapes and Olives

Today is vintage time. Beneath Émbonas you can wander through vineyards and olive groves. The three-hour circular walk ends with a slight ascent. Except for the grapes you pluck yourself, there is no chance to get refreshments.

AWT 0.00 In front of the **"Ataviros" Hotel** (or "Vassilia") you leave the asphalt road downhill and, after a stream bed, wander along a narrow dirt path through several olive groves ①.

0.07 At the **fork**, the way continues uphill to the left, then along a steeper cement path. After a hilltop, you look over

0.15 a wide valley lined with woods. At a right-angled **turn-off to the right**, a few metres before another fork, you go downhill and immediately onto the narrower path to the right, which soon makes a curve to the left. If it ends up at an overgrown spot, continue through an olive grove, climbing downhill over the terraces until you come to a

0.25 **dirt path** above a vineyard. Here you continue to the right, with the valley on your left, until you meet up with a wider road, which you walk along downhill to the left,

0.30 under **electric wires** until you come to a **crossing**.

At this point you turn sharply to the right onto a narrow dirt road and walk, in a curve to the left, to a vineyard with a footpath along its right edge. Go downhill along it

0.35 and to the left in front of a small hill to reach a **dirt path** leading downhill through a ditch. At the next fork, turn to the left and then, where the paths cross, continue straight on! You have reached the lower edge of the vineyard region of Émbonas, bordered on the left by the gorge

of the river Lireno, with pines growing along the cliffs. Wander for a longer while and don't let the turn-offs to the right or left bother you. You don't turn off until you

0.55 come to a **crossing of the paths** ② , where you turn to the right towards the ascent. At the next fork, too, continue uphill to the right. In a hollow you see a reservoir and on the coast the greenhouses of Kamirós-Skála. In the direction you are heading, Atáviros arises, the highest mountain on the Dodecanese. Grapes grow all around you, so many that you have no chance of tasting all of them. A

1.10 **pump house** is to the left of the path. After reached the
1.20 top, you return to the wine village of **Émbonas**.

Those thirsting for knowledge can now walk another eight minutes to the left along the edge of the village to the Emery vineyard (or turn off earlier to the small Kounaki vineyard) and can ask questions about the viticulture here until 4 p.m. while tasting wines.

At first glance, the **wine village of Émbonas** doesn't appear to be very inviting. In the old section above the main thoroughfare, however, there are a lot of nice corners and little old houses. In the evening, when the tour buses have long since returned home, the locals and the few visitors meet in the tavernas for a leisurely meal and more wine-tasting.

▶ **Hotel Ataviros** (Tel. 22460-41235). The innkeeper, Kyriakos, is glad to help if you have any problems with transportation.

⑤ An Alpine Tour to Mount Atáviros

This tour should only be taken by somewhat experienced mountain wanderers. The rather steep climb through treeless fields of boulders  demands good physical condition, but there aren't any dizzying heights to make you feel giddy. The difference in altitude is about 800 m. There are no cisterns, so you should be well equipped - also with protection from the wind and a pair of long pants. You should plan six hours for the tour and choose a good day since the danger of fog should not be underestimated.

AWT 0.00 On the left side of the street leading west in **Émbonas** there is a **wine tasting room** which you should rather pass by at the moment. After the curve, take the road in

0.02 front of the **storage area** uphill to the left through the vineyard terraces. This is where the *Villaré* grows, the best white wine on Rhodes. The road narrows down to a path which meets up with another path. On this new path you should walk to the right and then to the left right away. Below a stone wall , turn steeply uphill to the left, through chunks of boulders. Cairns show you the way. There is a hut in the vineyard on the right. Shortly after

0.25 this, climb over a fence using a **ladder** and walk along to the right above the fence to another ladder and then from there continue uphill. After the last red markings, battle your way upwards through the field of boulders or climb up through the rocks on the right. Further up, dead electric wires serve as a security line in the rubble. You will be

1.10 happy to reach the **edge of the cliff** at the upper end of

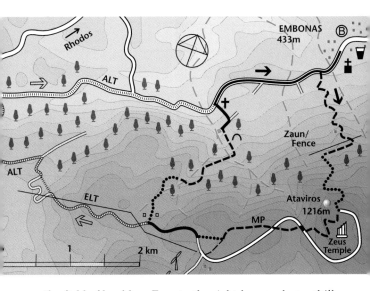

the field of boulders. Turn to the right here and go uphill
1.30   between the rocks ③ to the **peak** with the measurement
column globular telecommunication construction. This is
the highest point in the Dodecanese at 1215 m – hopefully with a good view! People say you can see to Crete on a
clear day. Every few years there is even snow here.
1.35   To the south you can see the base of an old **temple to
Zeus** on the next hill and can reach it quickly without a
path. There are not even pillars left, although this is actu-
ally to be expected in Greece.
Shortly before the sea, you discover an old foot path
down to the street. Behind the hills there are wind rotors.
1.50   Continue downhill to the **street** in zigzag lines and then
out of the hollow diagonally uphill to the right on the
other side of the street but over to the side a bit. Then you
cross over the street again and wander leisurely over the
hill and amiably downhill. It is a lovely old wandering
path, with the signs of the times in the background. A dirt
track has been built below this path, and you can get
down to it without a path at the best spot. After a few
2.20   curves along this **dirt track**, you come to a plateau fur-
2.25   ther down, and you see the **ruins of houses** (right) ④,
100 m *in front of the electric wires*.

Alternative: The following description is of an old foot path which hardly anyone, even the locals, knows about any more. For the first 25 minutes it is quite hard to find in the Phrýgana and the boulders. It continues down as a rocky path and is easier to find.

The alternative is to use the wide dirt track down to the street (AWT 3.20), then to try to get a ride in a car or to walk along the street for 4–5 km to reach Émbonas.

2.25 After the **ruins** walk in the slight hollow at first. There are some new (!) orange markings. Then continue about 50 m left of the ditch and hop over the rocks. You can see Ém-

2.45 bonas. Later the ditch on the right is full of **pines**. From here on, you continue levelly at first and then downhill to the right – with a mountain ridge to your left – through the pines. Now there are more parts of the old path which

2.55 **cross through the gorge** in a curve to the right. The val-

★ ley bed is to the left now, and a wildly romantic mountain path begins. It leads downhill and almost reaches the bottom of the gorge three minutes later. From here it continues almost levelly again across slabs of rock. Then it leads slightly downhill to the left towards a rock wall which is

3.10 hollowed out at the bottom. At the **caves**, shuffle downhill to the left through the large rocks. Where the two

3.15 gorges meet there is a **watering place for livestock**. You pass through a gate here, walk downhill to the left at the

3.20 fork to reach the **street** and continue along it to the right. If you can't find a helpful driver, at least you have the opportunity to try the grapes in fall as you meander along

3.40 the street to **Émbonas**.

Why not try out the *Villaré* in the wine-tasting room while you are at it?

⑥ Mountain Meadows beneath the Akramítis

A shady path leads up to the Akramítis massif and crosses through beautiful park-like meadows. You can wander on past the chapel of Saint John up to the peak. After a somewhat steep descent, you return to the street near Siána. No functioning cisterns can be found during the three to four hours of walking. At four places you must pay careful attention to the turn-offs!!

AWT 0.00 0.10 First look at the clock at the **taverna** "Christos Corner", then walk up the street and 10 minutes later you will notice a **parking area** on the right side of the street. Across from it yellow cairns (piled stones) ① mark the way up the slope. In the woods turn left after 50 m at the cairn

!! 0.18 and then walk up the easily seen path. Another cairn later marks the **turn-off** up to the right ②.

⑦ *continues straight on.*

The walk continues upwards, at first with a bit of effort, then later very pleasantly between the pines, with a lovely view of the broad Apolakkía Bay. At the **end of the ascent**, wander down through the pine woods and then on

0.35

0.40 ★ the right of a ravine to a wonderful **glade** ③, where all of Greece's flowers bloom in spring, between age-old pines and cedars, ruins and decaying trees – a romantic painter like William Turner would probably have reached quickly for his sketch pad.

You ascend a few metres through violet sage blooms and cross over a stone wall which used to surround a field.

1 2

From the other side of the wall it is only 200 paces until a
1.00 phalanx of **cairns** direct the wanderer uphill to the right
!! and not straight on along the wider goat path. When you
have passed the cliff, a wide meadow stretches out in
front of you, in which, to the left and barely perceptible,
1.05 there is the chapel **Ayios Ioannis**. The structure is plain
except for the lovely frescoes in the old apse. Even just its
situation in this abandoned area makes seeing it an experience.

Alternative: The rest of the way on down to Siána is un-
even and bumpy. You could also consider returning
the same way you came through the lovely meadows.
On the other side of the meadow a reddish-coloured path

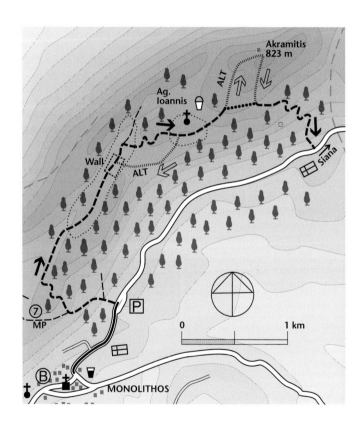

leads slowly up to an open mountain pasture with a pine grove above it ④. There is a quaint **cairn** to the right of the path, directly in front of a tree trunk.

1.11
!!

>*Alternative:* It is only 10 minutes straight ahead to the observation station for forest fires near the **peak of the Akramítis** (823 m). By clear weather the view is very worthwhile. A path also leads into the valley from there.

1.11 If you turn right at the cairn, you will find a goat path over the hill and can walk downhill slowly from there, without a path, staying to the left until you reach a wide,

1.20 red **footpath**, which you follow downhill. Soon there are

1.25 **ruins** 100 m to the right between pines. The path becomes steeper but shadier. Far down below you turn left at

1.45 a cairn on a boulder to reach the **street**.

It is 30 minutes on foot down to **Monólithos**; hitch-hiking is only 5 minutes.

It takes eight minutes uphill to reach **Siána**, with its narrow lanes and nice little tavernas. The village is famous for honey, yoghurt and especially Zúmo- a kind of grappa.

❼ The Hidden Cave

This two-hour tour branches off of walk ⑥ after 18 minutes, leads along a well-cared-for path to a romantic rest point with beautiful view and then from there on to a hidden cave.

AWT 0.18   Follow ⑥ until AWT 0.18 (picture ②) and, when you come to the **fork**, continue walking *straight ahead* uphill along *the wider path* ①, with the broad bay of Apolakkías to your left. The path has been improved again by the community and leads, without any problems, past a

0.25   **round threshing area**, an Alóni, and then to a **moun-**
0.30   **tain ridge**. Sitting on a stone you can enjoy the beautiful view of the peninsula of Armenistís and the island of Chálki lying in front of you.

From there you continue to the right along a wildly romantic path and at its end turn right onto narrow curves
0.40   leading steeply upwards to a **memorial plaque**. Above it to the left you can see the entrance to a cave.

Resistance fighters hid in this cave during the war and stayed in radio communication with the British. A young woman secretly took care of them and brought the most important news as well as food, which she carried up along various hidden paths. She died just a few years ago. For those who don't want to get dirty, a photo of the cave hangs above the fireplace in the restaurant "Liméri".

⑧ Monólithos

On this five-hour walking tour you circle at a respectful distance round the crusade citadel enthroned on a steep cliff. There are several possibilities for taking a swim and then a terrific sunset at the end. The length of the tour is, however, 7 km, so you might want to take a short cut in the middle.

AWT
0.00

You should take some water for your walk at the lovely **village fountain** in **Monólithos** since there is no possibility along the way to get refreshments. Then, keeping to the left, meander downhill along the street above the gardens and turn to the right at the last houses ① onto a cement path which is soon flanked on the left with natural walls of loess. It leads through terraces of olive trees and straight down to the valley floor. Here you turn right

0.09

onto the **country road** and follow it uphill after a bridge.

!!
0.15

At the fork, go to the left – don't miss the somewhat overgrown **dirt road** leading *downhill to the left* after an olive grove – now nothing can go wrong for the moment.

0.20
0.35

At the end of the road, walk to the right past the grape vines and then take a half-right between two fields of grain to the right edge of the forest, where you unknot and refasten the **gate**. You will find a sufficient number of red dots in the sparse pine forest to reach the **edge of the forest** soon. Charred tree trunks from the fire in 1999 stand in front of the sea. Since it is easy to lose your way in the next part of the walk, you are recommended to take the bright rocky peninsula on the right of the broad

1.00   mountain ridge ② as your goal. The **sandy beach of Foúrni** lies to the right at the end of the way.

> *There are several **caves** on the peninsula's steep east sandstone coast. Some of these are said to be over 1000 years old. Beneath the stony remains of the light tower on the point, there is a cruciform cave church in which a grave was found*

The wide beach is not visited frequently. At the end of the wider part, the way continues between pines along the as-

1.10   phalt street until you arrive at the next (smaller) **beach**. Now the way becomes fairly strenuous as you go on uphill along the street. At the top, to the left of the street, there is a rock formation in the shape of a dragon, like the one

1.35   slain by Saint George. It marks the **sandy path** leading downhill to the left behind it.

> **Short Cut:** Follow the asphalt street up to Monólithos. Continue along the sandy path to the left, from which a turn-off leads down to the left to a bay with the island of Strongli (= the round one).

Your straight path offers beautiful views of Cape Armenistís and, behind that, the island of Chálki, as you walk down along it. After a curve to the right you can look

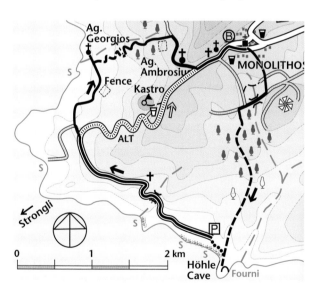

up to Mount Akramítis, to the small white chapel halfway up (where you will still go today!) and to the rocky monolith with the citadel, whose walls seem to grow out of the cliff. 80 m after a **vineyard** (on the right) you can begin looking for the way up further ③ and wander on to the chapel of **Ayios Georgios**.

2.00

2.05

> *The interior is decorated in a rustical manner; the dragon killer rides along the wall to the right. In front there is a shady spot for a picnic, with a bell made from a grenade shell – divine. And down below, a mini-bay!*

Along the way back, you must be very careful not to miss the **turn-off** ③ to the left with the cairns, which comes just 4 minutes later. An old, somewhat decayed path meanders uphill, turns to the right, then leads on upwards, crosses a fence twice and ends at the beginning of a **dirt road**. This leads along flat ground to the left and then up through pines to a **glade** with olives and grape wines. From there continue on uphill to the right to a flat, wide dirt track and then to the right again, past the Ambrosius Chapel to the asphalt street.

2.09

!!

2.25

2.40

> *The romantically inclined now walk downhill to the right for 12 minutes to the **Monólithos citadel** ④ and enjoy the famous **panorama at sunset**.*
>
> *Always a place of asylum and a fortress, a citadel of the Order of Saint John stood here beginning in 1476. Only the remains of the wall are left over. The chapel of Saint Panteléimon was added on later.*

The others can turn off to the left to end the day in the taverna "**Panorama**". Each decision has its advantages.

3.05

▶ **Hotel** in Monólithos: »Thomas«, Tel.: 2 24 60-612 91.

⑨ Asklipío

Untouched by tourism, the village of Asklipío enchants the visitor with its white houses and narrow lanes. The wonderful frescoes in the church of Mary's Passing Away are absolute jewels. This three-hour walk leads there along pebble paths, offers a broad panorama view of the sea on the way back and ends at a lovely sandy beach. You must get off the bus from Rhodes/Lindos shortly before Gennádi!

AWT **Shortly after the big beach hotels of Kiotári**, there is a petrol station on the right. 200 m later a bridge follows, and then, after another 200 m, you must ask the bus driver to stop. A sandy path leads away from the street here and

0.00 into the interior of the island, past an **electric transforming station** and accompanied by power lines. You pass by

0.07 a deteriorating **water pump** (right) and keep to the right at a fork but then turn left at the next. Then the path continues slightly uphill, with the massive cement wall of a

0.15 gravel-pit to the right. At the next **fork**, turn to the right onto the plains of the Katáchra River. On the other side

0.35 you can see the village of Asklipío on the slope. The **turn-off** to the right leads through the dry stream bed, then to the left and later uphill. Continue below a chapel and on past a fountain, and soon, after a curve, you are greeted by the broadly sprawling white village ①. Beneath the village, you pass by gardens, cross the asphalt street and walk up-

1.00 hill along the narrow, twisting lanes to **Asklipío**. After walking beneath the bell tower, you come to the famous chapel **Kímissi tis Theotókou**.

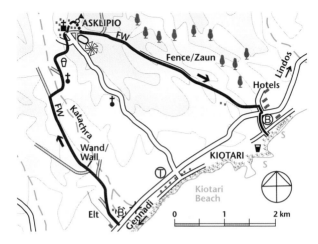

The chapel is dedicated to Mary's Ascension to Heaven or Passing Away and has the most beautiful frescoes on Rhodes. The original chapel from 1060 had the shape of a Latin cross and was later expanded with side aisles. The central area was painted in the 17th century. In the middle of the nave you see the genesis, the creation of the world. In the right transept the Revelation of Saint John, in the left transept pictures from the life of Christ.

First walk along the lane to the right of the cafe "Platía", then look for the way up to the **castle ruins** ②. Much from the Order of Saint John is there: the gate, a cistern, battlements. There is a beautiful view over land and sea. From up on top, aim for the sports field, which you can reach without a path, walking between olive trees. The sandy sports field should stay to your right beneath the road. At the next **fork**, turn downhill to the right and stay on the wider path at the subsequent turn-offs. The fence to the left serves to keep the wild forest goats away from the fields. Walk on towards the sea in wide, gentle curves. The **clay pigeon shooting range** remains on your right, as you walk along a **street** leading downhill to the right to reach the **bus stop** in front of the Hotel "Rhodos Maris". You can find a spot in the sand on the beach. The wanderer needn't pay attention to the animators' shouts of encouragement accompanying the sports activities. Instead, you can laze on the beach until the bus arrives.

1.10
1.15
1.40
2.00
2.05

⑩ Moní Tharí

Anyone who wants to wander through the Greek forests at some time should take this three to four-hour tour. You walk to the famous St. Michael's Cloister in Tharí along roads which aren't too steep and then return to Laérma in a wide loop. You will only find water in Tharí.
The only bus connection to Laérma is in the afternoon, so you should plan either to spend the night (see below) or to go from Lárdos by taxi or by hitching a ride.

AWT
0.00   After the **Church of Laérma** (right), you pass by the restaurant "Igkos" (left) on the slightly ascending street, then turn off the street to the left 200 m later after a right curve and walk along a dirt road leading downhill and
0.11   lined with pine and olive trees. At the **fork**, continue straight on downhill and down below in the flat area,
0.15   turn to the **right**. Meander light-footed, passing by the
0.25   **turn-off** (to the left), and you will come to a military depot (right) shortly. At the fork, bear to the left downhill and then directly afterwards to the right and on through a
0.30   **stream bed**, which can carry water until May.

At the following fork, go uphill to the left and then
0.50   through the wooded hillside to the **cloister of Tharí** ①.

This cloister, dedicated to the archangel Michael, is a forging tool for the Orthodox Church. The 15–20 monks living here will come far in the church hierarchy – so it is said. The cloister also sends forth missionaries.
Visitors can view the old, completely painted church,

whose oldest, 600-year-old frescoes are in the altar area. Saint Michael can be seen several times, with his sword in the right hand and a child in the left. He is fighting against the powers of darkness with his sword and accompanies mankind's souls, symbolically represented by the child, into eternity. One special portrayal is the representation of Christ sitting.

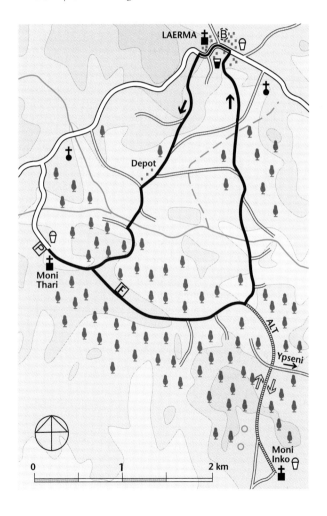

Return briefly along the way you came, and then continue on uphill to the right at the fork above the cloister church. On the left of the ridge, you can see Atáviros, the highest mountain on Rhodes (1215 m) ②. The dirt path was cleared to make a lane for fire protection, and soon

1.05 you come to a fire **observation station** along the way. In 1987 and 1992 there were devastating forest fires here.

1.15 At the **crossing of the paths** ③, follow the sign "Inko" straight on. The delightful smell of pine trees makes your hike much easier. Pay no regard to a turn-off to the right,

1.35 but instead take the **turn-off to the left** which follows.

> *Alternative:* If you are still full of energy, you can continue straight on for a quarter of an hour to **Cloister Inko** with its church to Saint George ④. The way there leads on further along the wide fire lane. The chapel has old furnishings, but the exterior renovation is extremely obvious. There is a cistern.

1.35 After the **turn-off to the left**, you come to a narrower forest path leading downhill. Pay no attention to two turn-offs to the right. Just enjoy the walk down to the valley along this wonderful path through the pines. The village of Laérma is located at the edge of the woods.

1.55 Walk or wade through the **dry stream bed** or the stream again. You will pass by lovely Greek farmland before you

2.30 can order a good Greek salad in **Laérma**.

▶ **Spending the night:** The inn-keeper of the "Igkos" restaurant can arrange for rooms. He speaks English and German. Tel.: 2 24 40-6 10 71.

⑪ Líndos

This walking tour is the loveliest way to get to Lín-dos, except for taking a boat trip. You walk amidst olive trees and oaks along well-marked goat tracks. You cross over a mountain ridge and arrive, without great exertion, in Líndos after two and a half to three hours. There is no place to get water along the approximately eight kilometres.

AWT
0.00

The bus station is located above **Vlichá** before the **fork in the road**. From there it is about 200 m along the street to Líndos until you come to a bridge, but before it turn right onto a dirt road which leads downhill amidst olive trees to a dry stream bed. On the other side of the stream, continue uphill to the right without a path through terraces of olive trees towards the rock wall. Later, on the flat land, walk to the left across a dirt way and through a dry stream

0.15

bed again, until you come to a **road**. After a gate, it arrives at an impressive gully ① ② lined with pines. Before the

0.30

road leads to the right through the dry bed, take a **path** straight ahead marked by cairns – leaving the dry stream bed on the right and the road behind it. The path comes to a wide hollow where there is an olive grove on the left and a cave can be seen straight ahead on the slope. You

0.40

cannot enter this **cave** since it is used as a siesta spot by a large herd of goats. Anyway, the classics expert knows that a Cyclops sometimes resides in Greek caves.

Above the cave, you continue going uphill slightly through sharp rocks, between which inquisitive "stone men", the cairns, look out curiously ③. Kermes oaks pro-

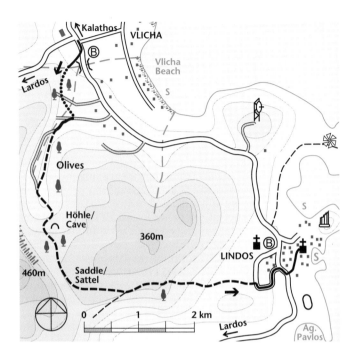

vide shade for the path, which meanders somewhat to the right along the bottom of the mountain. Once you have come to the **ridge**, you head downhill. At the end of the high plateau which comes next, you can see the sea again. Further down, the path leads to the left along a hardly visible path which is accompanied by a dry wall. The lovely view across the sea and up to a chapel on a peak should not draw your attention away from the cairns! They lead to an **elevation** from which the ancient acropolis of Líndos can finally be seen. The huddled old little houses in the hollow are still not visible. A fitting, shady rest area awaits you on the right.

0.50

1.20

The rest can be told quickly. Pay no attention to the new buildings on the left and look forward to the lovely hilly lanes in **Líndos** ④.

1.50

▶ **Swimming:** If you want to swim first, walk along the main street another 5 min. to the bay of the apostle Paul.

⑫ Crusader Castles

During this lovely four-hour walk along the coastline, you have the opportunity to visit the ruins of two crusader castles. In between, there is magnificent coastal scenery and several sandy beaches. However, the well-marked path demands a bit of physical fitness

AWT   The point of departure is the **castle** above the village of **Archángelos**. The defensive bulwark has been restored, but there is nothing remaining from the interior.

0.00   Beneath the castle, on the side towards the city, walk along the cement road away from the **steps** toward the south, with the city on your right hand side. It is like an oasis sur-

0.04   rounded by barren countryside. Before the few **houses** on the ridge, look for a way on the left through the rocks. From the other side of the small ridge ①, a rather wide path leads down to the olive trees and into the valley. Be-

0.10   hind this **grove**, go along a dirt road to a wider sandy track and walk along it to the left. Three minutes later, change your direction in a sharp angle to the right and walk through the charming farming countryside towards the

0.25   sea. At a **fork**, go to the right and then shortly afterwards

!!   *to the right again at the cairns* onto a narrow footpath. Soon you will see the holiday village of Stegná, which has developed quite a bit in the last few years – you can hear this through the animators' loudspeakers.

0.40   The path goes downhill in an arc between the rocks **above Stegná**. Wander to the right along the plateau, towards the south ②. A dirt path to the right of the fences

leads to a rocky path which can be seen from afar and
0.55 mounts to a **ridge**.

From there, continue downhill to the left along the wider
dirt road to the water and turn right at a fork. Bizarre
caves in the boulders on the left are used as a shelter by
the goats. After passing between several simple holiday
1.15 houses, you arrive at the **Bay of Klisoúras**.

Behind the fenced-in houses, take the track to the west,
and you will arrive at a long rectangle cut into the rocks:
an **ancient quarry**, as you can still see by the steps. The
stones for Líndos, which is located opposite this area,
were probably hewn here.

On the other narrow side of the rectangle, a red dot directs you into a beautiful rocky landscape ③. Walk left
along the dirt road you come to later until you reach the
old olive tree and then find the continuation of the foot

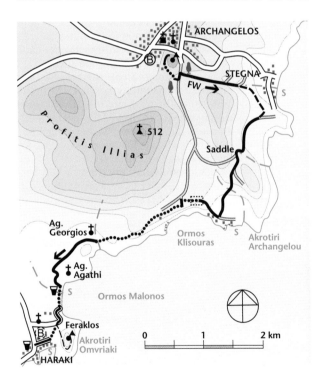

1.40   path after 20 m. A **little house** made of quarry stones stands alone on the plateau. Far below, decorated with flags and crosses, there is a wonderful beach under the cliff, and a steep path before you get to the little house leads down to it. Your path continues on the right of the

1.50   little house. You can avoid a somewhat **steep area** by go-
✓ ing above it to the right (red dots). Then the landscape
★ plays another trump. In the summer you can do a slalom run between the rocks and thistles, which are as tall as a man. If you look back, you can see a gigantic rock gate which makes you think of Salvador Dalí ④. To the right, you can see the chapel to Saint George. The wanderer is

2.05   crammed through a **double fence** and then continues

2.20   along a dirt path around a stone hill to the **sandy bay of Agáthi** with its lively beach, refreshment establishments and chapel (have you found it?). The bay is surrounded by ruins of castles and other structures. You must briefly share the dirt track with cars and motor bikes until you come to the sign to the castle.

> The **castle of Féraklos**, once built on top of an ancient acropolis, was torn away from Byzantium by the Order of Saint John in 1306 and was their first and most powerful citadel on Rhodes.
> It wasn't until after a long Turkish siege that it was captured in 1523, after the fall of the city of Rhodes. Little remains except for the embattlements.

The ascent is steep, and, if the ruins of one castle a day are enough for you, you can easily find your way through the meadows and on past an archaeological area (left) to

2.35   **Charáki**. Here you can see what can be made out of a "romantic little fishing village on a protected bay".

⑬ The Cloister of Tsambíka

This cloister, located on a peak 340 m high, is the destination for many pilgrims and the climax of to-day's walk, First you can swim at the most beautiful beach on Rhodes – Tsambíka Beach. The walk is not strenuous except for the ascent through the rocky terrain to the cloister. You can get refreshments at the beach as well as near the cloister. The starting point is the second largest city on the island, Archángelos, which can easily be reached by bus.

AWT

0.00

0.05

0.10

0.20

The street to Stégna leads eastwards from the main street in Archángelos, next to a cemented stream bed. On the other (northern) side of the stream bed there is a **taxi stand**. From there, go along the street towards the sea, on the left of the dry bed. Three minutes later go straight ahead and leave the street, walking directly along the stream bed. Then take the **road uphill to the left** to several pens. To the right, the mountain of the prophet Elijah arises and, in front of it, the crusader castle's long wall. From the pens, walk **through a valley** in an arc to the right and look for a dirt path off to the left on the next low hill. At the subsequent fork in the little forest, bear to the right and, at a collection of indescribable variety representing a Greek farm pen, continue uphill to the **asphalt street.** Go downhill to the right along this street for a short while and then uphill to the left at a small private chapel. Now you can see today's destination on a steep mountain: the cloister of Tsambíka. Behind the garden surrounding a large house, turn to the right and walk,

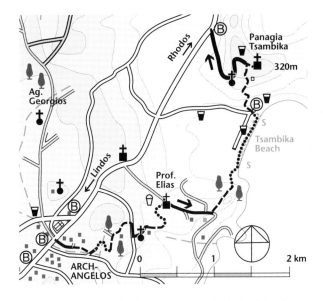

possibly through a chicken fence, on the left of the fence straight on downhill towards the sea. From here there is a magnificent panorama view of the cloister on the cliff and the sandy bay located in front of it ①.

0.40 Further down, walking without a path and keeping to the left through the hollow filled with olive trees and then going uphill, you reach the small **cloister of Profitis Elias** in a garden. It is, however, usually closed, so meander downhill along the dirt path next to the cloister wall and then bear left at the fork. Further down, don't take the left turn-off next to the olive garden but continue straight on towards the sea for a short while before you

0.50 turn **to the left** several metres before some **small rocks**. Your way continues *directly on the right edge of the olive grove* - not in the Phrýgana. A foot path leads from the lower corner of the grove through a sparse pine forest ② to a slope with fine sand ③. Swing downhill in an elegant

1.05 slalom to the **sandy beach of Tsambíka**. Take the sand out of your shoes, change your clothes, have a break! As you continue walking along the beach, you can decide whether you want to make the rest of the day easier and just hike to the bus stop. If not, look for the water pipes

1.15   on the left of the **shop at the bus stop**. They run diagonally uphill to the left along the ground ④. Follow them a few metres, then, before the pens, turn upwards to the right at a right angle. Cairns are awaiting you! A mighty boulder is located to the left of the steep path.

1.25   At the top you come to a **flatter stretch** and walk to the left across the cliff almost levelly. Then you turn steeply uphill to the right again, with a steep boulder on your left. Climb uphill in wide curves to a spot on the left where you have to cross over a boulder. If you have a great fear of heights, you must keep looking towards the right for five metres – but everyone manages. As a reward, you have a magnificent picnic spot right away. Down below is the beach and its little restaurants, which have staked out their claims.

1.50   After a sparse pine forest, you reach **ruins** (right) and
1.55   steps leading uphill to the left to the **parking lot**. You will share the remaining 297 steps with panting car drivers
2.05   until you reach the **cloister of Tsambíka**, the cloister of Our Dearly Beloved Virgin.

> *The guest is met by a small courtyard. There are some accommodations for women who wish to bear children: a night on the mountain is said to have helped even in difficult cases. That's why a lot of photographs of healthy little children can be seen on the left wall of the chapel. Saint Charámbolos looks very old in comparison.*

The **walk down** the steps leads to the restaurant with its wonderful terrace, where you can sit as if you were in a quiet Alpine meadow and look down upon the gigantic hotels in Kolímbia. You can smile hopefully at a car driver here or else walk down along the street for 15 minutes
2.30   and hop onto the bus on the **main street**.

Crusades

Jerusalem, sacred to Jews, Moslems and Christians, had been in Arabian possession since 637, but Christian pilgrims were always welcome. Entry to the city was not the reason for the crusades. The militant reform movement coming from Cluny strove for an increase in the Pope's power. It was very convenient that Pope Urban II was asked by the Eastern Roman Empire in 1095 to help against the Seljuks, who were pressing forward from Asia. The charismatic Pope succeeded in mobilizing great masses of people. The original 40,000 people became more than 130,000, with every tenth one of them a noble knight. Piety and a passion for glory were the main reasons for participation; there was little to gain materially. Processions, prayers and fasting were practiced during the crusades.

At the same time, the Jews were being persecuted in Europe and accused of being guilty of Christ's crucifixion

The first crusade was the only successful one. At the time, the Islamic opponents were weakened by the split into Sunnites and Shiites. Jerusalem was conquered in 1099, and the knights killed 70,000 people – Mohammedans, Jews and even Christians. Jerusalem then became a Christian kingdom. Settlements grew up along the coasts, but there were too few settlers and the country could not be controlled from the citadels alone. The Seljuks reconquered the city of Edessa in 1144, which lead to the second, totally unsuccessful crusade.

In 1187 the Saracens under Sultan Saladin tore the kingdom of Jerusalem away from the Christians again. A gigantic new army was set up for the third crusade and led by the German emperor Friedrich I. Barbarossa, the later English king Richard the Lion-Hearted, the French king Philip II and Leopold I from Austria. They were only able to reconquer Akkon. After Barbarossa had drowned, the armies of crusaders returned home.

The fourth crusade (1201–1204) did not achieve its actual goal of conquering Egypt but ended in the sacking of the Christian city of Constantinople. Venice had incited the crusaders to destroy it due to trading rivalries.

Three more unsuccessful crusades, none of which were led with full strength, took place before 1270. At the same time, Christian armies drove the Moslems out of Spain and christianised the Slaws in Prussia and in the Baltic.

After 1300 the knighthoods had to withdraw from the mainland of Asia Minor to the islands situated in front of it, but they were chased away from there, too, by the Turks in 1523.

Κάρπαθος
Kárpathos

The very narrow and mountainous island of Kárpathos is the second largest of the Dodecanes. At the narrowest spot, the island is only four kilometres wide, but it is ten times as long. Along with its sister islands Kássos and Saría, it rises up on a broad undersea base which stretches from the Greek mainland to Turkey. The sea falls off to a depth of 2500 metres on both sides. Tourism has been established in the flat southern section, where the airport is also located. The guests, not yet too many in number, can find all categories of overnight accommodations and the corresponding leisure activities here. Although tourism is the main source of income, it does not dominate everything. Road construction has thus been carried out with a certain sense of proportion. The wanderer is more attracted to the middle of the island and to its northern part. These regions are counted among the most beautiful walking areas in the Aegean. You can walk through shady pine forests, olive groves and magnificent rocky landscape along old mule tracks to get to chapels and villages which have only recently been supplied with electric current. Here you can occasionally listen to music played on archaic instruments like the lyre and lute and accompanied by spontaneous singing as you try the island's excellent specialities. Unfortunately there were forest fires in some regions in 1982 and 1990, but the traces of these are now slowly healing. Walks 18 and 22 can also be done as a day's excursion by boat starting out from Pigádia.

⑭ Along Old Paths to Lefkós

This easy three-hour walk leads down from Mesochóri to the beautiful beaches in Lefkós. You wander mainly along old foot paths which are counted among the loveliest still preserved and lead through shady pine forests. There are tavernas at the beginning and the end as well as a fountain along the way.
Getting to Mesochóri can be problematic. Take the morning bus towards Lefkos, but get off in Ay. Geórgios already. It takes an hour along the street to get to Mesochóri if a friendly driver doesn't give you a lift. There are no taxis.

AWT Get a supply of fresh spring water below the main church in **Mesochóri** and meander a bit through the lanes of the lovely village. At the southern end of the houses, there is

0.00 a **church** ① with a tile roof, and the old path begins below it on the right. Immediately afterwards it turns to the

0.03 right, and then at the next **fork** you bear to the left. Stroll between old stone walls enclosing olive groves and gardens, with the sea on your right. At another fork, bear

★   to the left. A fairy tale landscape with old, well-preserved

0.20 paths encircles the wanderer ②. **Steps** lead to a mountain ridge ③ from which you can cast a last look at Mesochóri. On the other side of the hill, cross over a dirt road to

0.30 reach half-grown pines. A **path through the woods** and next to electric wires leads you over a plateau. The peak of Profitis Elias (1168 m) arises exactly 1000 m above you. At

0.40 the end of the forest path, you descend into a **valley** and, on the other side, walk uphill through a shady forest

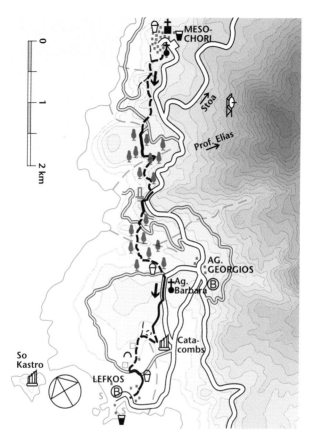

along a wide Kalderími, a flagstone path, for quite a while
0.55 until you come to the **street**. Here you turn to the right,
then at the fire observation tower to the right again and
finally 15 m later downhill to the left onto a dirt road.

1.00 At the first pines, cairns point out the way **downhill to
the right**. Here you meet up with the old flagstone path
again, which soon crosses with a forest path. Diagonally
opposite on the left, look for more markings on a narrow
path through a sparse pine forest.

1.25 After a short climb you come to a **fountain** on the right
and then immediately afterwards a small asphalt street,
which you should wander along straight on, with the

Barbara Chapel on the left and the houses from the scattered settlement of Ayios Geórgios in the fields. 200 m after the chapel, follow the signs pointing to the right to the Roman cistern. At the end of the dirt road, before the garden enclosed by stones on the right, you will see the

1.40 **Roman cisterns** on the left, a few steps away.

> *It is still in dispute whether these are cisterns or catacombs. It is only certain that the underground room, which is supported by 15 pillars, dates back to Roman times.*

From here, return a few steps the way you came. Before the parking area, turn to the left onto a foot path and then later to the left again onto a wider path through a barren, stony heath landscape and leading to a small hill.

1.50 Below the **water reservoir** (right), a monopáti begins to lead downhill. After a few minutes, you can see the **cave** on the right.

> *As shown by the remains of shells on the ceiling, it was most probably under the sea, then pushed upwards and used by mankind since immemorial times. Wall niches on the sides could have been graves. The walls, which were later built as animal pens, make this place extremely fascinating.*

From the cave, continue downhill, taking a left at the water tank, then a right at the next crossing and arriving

2.05 down at one of the **beaches in Lefkós** . And now just jump into the water.

> *In the times of early history, a city populated by 30,000 people was located here. It was protected by the fortress Só Kastro, on the steep island situated in front of it, where many remains still await the archaeologists' diggings.*

⑮ Kalí Límni, the Beautiful Lake

No one knows where this name for a mountain comes from. "Beautiful" is right in any case. This seven to eight-hour walk is strenuous but unforgettable. In addition to long, almost flat stretches, there is the steep climb up to Kalí Límni, with its 1215 m the highest mountain on the Dodecanese – next to Atáviros on Rhodes. The wanderer sees the variety of landscapes on Kárpathos: its charming west side and the magnificently wild east coast.

You must, however, observe a few rules for this mountain walk. On days with strong cloud formations, there is the danger of losing your orientation on the mountain. Moreover, you must be especially protected against wind and sun. Perseverance is demanded, but you needn't be free of attacks of vertigo. Water is available at several places, and there is even a taverna at the foot of the mountain. A secret tip: take along swimming gear.

You can shorten the tour by 1½ hours and, for about nine euros, take a taxi from Pigádia to Lástos for the beginning part.

AWT   Take the bus to Voláda or have the driver let you out two minutes later at the turn-off to "Kalí Límmi" (see ALT on the map).

0.00   In **Voláda**, walk uphill at an apartment building ①, but then leave the steep road lined with walls three minutes later to turn left onto a foot path. Shortly afterwards, turn

0.05   right onto a **dirt road**, which ends unexpectedly in a

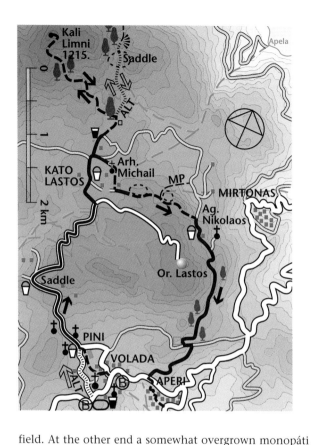

field. At the other end a somewhat overgrown monopáti awaits you and leads to a cement road. Continue along

0.12 this steeply uphill to the left until you come to the "**main street**". At the **fountain** there, take a right turn, still uphill, through the lovely high valley with the scattered houses of the hamlet Píni.

0.25 The little road goes across a **ridge**, where you can enjoy not only fresh spring water but also a wonderful view of the charming west coast all the way to Kássos. The walking route continues along the road, high above the coast. The view is occasionally breath-taking and makes you forget the asphalt. Today's destination, Kalí Límni, slowly comes into view, with the Lástos plateau ② beneath it to the right.

1.05 At the **fork**, the asphalt road leads uphill to the right to a
military installation, but you should walk to the left along
1.10 the sand to the houses on the **Lástos plateau** (750 m
above sea level). At the end of it, you can reserve a place
1.20 for later in the **taverna** with the inn-keeper Thanássis.
Take leave of the fruitful gardens and fields at the road on
the right of the taverna and turn to the left 100 m later at
1.25 a **solitary tree** ③.

> *Alternative:* On days when the view is only mediocre,
> you are recommended to forego the peak and choose
> the nicer path on the right of the tree through the
> landscape. It is marked in blue and leads through a
> wide high valley with few climbs and individual pines,
> on through another field encircled by stones and then
> to a **ridge** (950 m above sea level)/AWT 1.55 with
> bizarrely ragged pines. From here you can see the steep
> coast of the island's northern section. This path would
> lead on to Spóa, but this is where you turn back.

1.25 The dare-devils turn to the left/straight on at the **solitary
tree** and follow the red dots steeply uphill. Some beads of
sweat will dampen your brow before you reach a flatter
area with cushions of thorn bush and spiny spurge and
2.05 then a gully where a few small, intimidated **kermes oaks**
offer some shade. You are now more than 1000 m above
sea level. From here, continue uphill, slipping somewhat
in the sand, to reach the rocky wind-protective forma-
2.20 tions at the **peak of Kalí Límni**.

> *From 1215 m above sea level, you have a view of the en-
> tire island and, on clear days, can see as far as Rhodes
> and Crete.*

Return downhill by the same route, and take a look into

2.55	the pots and pans in the **taverna** before you rest under the shady leaves. And amaze the others with the swimming gear you have brought along.
	After the break, return along the way you came for a bit, but bear left towards Arh. Michaílis at the fork. At the
3.05	next fork, follow a sign indicating the **church** of the Archangel Michael to the right. On the wall opposite it on the left, there are dots and arrows in all colours pointing out your way down to the gully. In front of the wall on the opposite slope, continue to the left along a dirt path to a small oasis bedded into the stone desert ④. Walk above it to the right, still following the red dots. They lead
3.20	you safely between the boulders to a fenced-in **garden**. (A small, refreshing waterfall is hidden in the oleander on the left of it!)
	Continue slightly downhill to the right above the garden. The lower part of the Lástos plains are on the left. A beau-
★	tiful, gently rolling landscape spreads out beneath the high peak in the mild afternoon light.
	With so much harmony, however, it is easy to lose your way. In this case, walk downhill to the left through the boulders to the dirt road and continue to the right along it. If you are still on the right track, you will not meet up
3.45	with this **dirt road** until later, and then not on the plateau but further to the north, where it struggles along above the steep east coast. The next stretch offers magnificent views of the sea, views you will dream of at night. There is a spring in front of a farmhouse hanging on the mountain. After it, you can look down upon Kirá Panagiá and up to the radar eye on the Koto mountain. Later the
4.00	**little church** of Saint Nicholas (see page 1) awaits you below the path.
	Wander on through the sparse pine forest, and you will
4.30	soon see Pigádia and Apéri. At the fork by a **water tank**, the way home first goes downhill to the left and immediately afterwards to the right. After striding through a
4.45	**gravel quarry**, you reach the main road. From here it is
4.50	only 50 m to the left to get to the **steps** leading down
5.05	through the many gardens in **Apéri** to the **Bishop's church**. Since it is almost always closed, head directly for the taverna "Four Seasons" for your reinvigoration.

⑯ Another Profítis Elías

This walking tour takes four and a half hours and leads to a view across the Egyptian Sea and from there down 500 m in altitude to a lovely beach. The tour begins in the charming village of Apéri, which can easily be reached by bus or taxi.
The tour is moderately difficult to difficult along dirt roads and paths and sometimes without paths (long trousers are absolutely necessary). There are fountains in Apéri and on the beach as well as a cistern at the church on the peak. From May to October a taverna awaits you on the beach.
Short cut: If you want to chug back comfortably by boat from Achata, inform the excursion boat "Sofia" on the pier the evening before or by 9:30 a.m.

AWT
0.00
Below the **road bridge in Apéri** there is a fountain, and above it the charming taverna "Four Seasons". The Bishop's church is on the right behind it, below the through street. If you continue down on the small street, you walk around the island's secondary schools, which were built from contributions by emigrants to America, the "Americánis".
The small street leads across the hill and then to the right to the sport fields (left). The new green one must be watered daily. King Football lets the green grass and the subventions sprout.

0.10
The cemetery is on the right. Opposite, on the left – slightly higher – there is a **chapel** ⧄, there you leave the street to the left. You pass through terraces of olive trees on the narrow path uphill. On the ridge at the top, you see

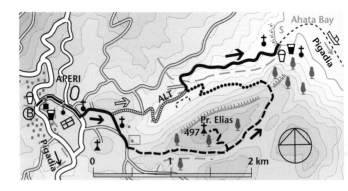

the destination, the apparently invincible mountain of
0.15 the prophet Elijah. A **dirt road turns off** to the left and
leads to a bay. For this, see the alternative route below.

But first you continue straight on, then slightly downhill
next to a chapel (left) and along a dirt road to the left un-
0.20 til you reach a rather new **pen** in a fenced-in area.

Directly afterwards, follow the arrows uphill to the left between boulders, sage, juniper bushes and shady pines to
0.45 the flat rear side of the mountain ②. On a green **plateau**
(390 m above sea-level), the path turns more steeply up-
1.00 hill to the left at the cairns to the **peak of Profitis Elias**
(500 m above sea-level).

> *The prophet Elijah, the Christian successor to the Greek
> sun god Helios, is the standard saint on the high island
> mountains closest to the sun. A small chapel can almost
> always be found on the peak of the mountain.*

The rest of the way can be seen clearly from here: fairly
exactly to the east and a bit lower, there is a wide gap and
behind it a plateau with trees. This is where the descent
down the steeper side of the mountain begins.

From the peak, return the way you came to get to the
1.15 **plateau** (AWT 0.45 for the ascent).

> *Alternative:* The way down to the bay described below
> is mainly without paths and somewhat steeper, but
> considerably shorter. If you want to go this way, you
> should be a little experienced in mountain walks but
> needn't be free of vertigo. There is a rather thorny
> stretch which cannot be walked through in shorts!

The **easier but longer way** to the bay leads back to

the right of the plateau along the same path for 40 minutes to AWT 0.15 and from there downhill to the right along dirt roads. It takes a total of 1.5 hours from the peak to the bay of Achata.

1.15 At the cairns (AWT 0.45), turn left onto a foot path which crosses the plateau and stay more on the left as you approach the side of the mountain. When the flat land begins to slope, walk uphill to the left along the incline. Red

1.30 dots lead to the **mountain gap** ③, with the trees you saw from on top. The church at the peak gives you the signal for your descent from the left at the top. Before that you could enjoy a pleasant picnic under the pines.

The way down begins on the right in the gap, continues down to the left, turns and goes to the boulders below and then from there to the left again to a few tall pines. From there continue downhill to the boulders and then walk a longer stretch to the left again. Shortly above the dry stream bed, a belt of very thorny bushes cuts off the direct path downhill. At this point you must press yourself direct-

2.20 ly against the bare rocks to reach the gully and the **dirt road** on the left of it without any wounds. What a relief! While you are walking down, look up at the cliff you have conquered, and you will feel like Edmond Hillary. The

2.50 other bathers at the **beach in Achata** ④ had an easier time getting here.

When Captain Vassilis zooms around the corner with his "Sofia", you needn't hurry. His other guests also dive into the clear water one more time before he steers his boat towards Pigádia.

Other possibilities: take the taxi you requested beforehand, hitchhike ... or return on foot!?!

⑰ A Day for Swimming

This will be a relaxing day. You take the gently curving stretch south of Diafáni along the coast for three hours – or even longer, with an extended stop for a swim. There is no chance to get refreshments along the way. Although you take the same way to return, it is never boring. Cairns mark the turn-offs from the dirt road.

AWT
0.00
On the hill above **Diafáni**, you can compare the techniques of the rigid Carpathian **windmills** to those of the common swinging ones. Walk in a left curve along a dirt road beneath the windmills, circling the little valley at the fishing port and passing two chapels (right).

When Cape Thalasopoúnda is on your left, leave the dirt road at the cairns, heading downhill to the left. After the trench you arrive back on the main road but soon leave it again to the left.

0.20
There is a lovely little **spot for swimming** in the hollow. If it is already occupied, walk up a footpath to a dirt road, which you will stay on for quite a while now. Then you go across another ditch ①. 100 m after a house (right), you cross through another valley. Once you are up out of it, the dirt road forks. *Not immediately*, but 30 m later, turn off to the left! The path leads to a hill above the sea. It becomes narrower here and meanders down into a wide val-

0.50
ley. The **beach of Papas Mínas** ② is on the left. If the dark grey slate slabs are too hot to lie on, you can cool them off with plastic bags full of sea water.

Go back the same way you came, but this time with a

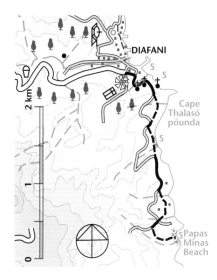

view of Mount Orkili (710 m). Shortly before Diafáni, turn-off to the right into the valley before the first chapel and enter the **harbour** with vim and vigour.

1.40

▶ The balconies of the fanciful **boarding house** "Glaros" are especially suitable for a lazy day (Tel. 224 50-515 01).

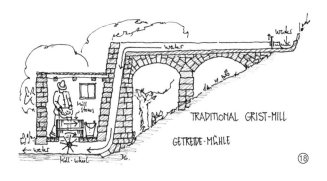

TRADITIONAL GRIST-MILL

GETREIDE-MÜHLE

⑱

⑱ A Day's Excursion

Especially those who come from Pigádia by ship for a day should "get a move on" for this walking tour. After visiting Ólympos, you can wander down to the ship in Diafáni in two hours.

This lovely route is comfortable and easy to find. In the beginning the course is identical with the last piece of walk 19, but in the opposite direction. There is a spring along the way.

AWT
0.00

Picturesque windmills are located along the edge of the slope in **Ólympos**, but the **taverna "Milos"** or "Windmill", built in at the bottom of the slope, is the only one to have covered blades. From here, go down several steps in an arc to the right, and you come to a dirt road on past the houses. Further downhill, turn off it to the left. Immediately afterwards, a foot path to the right leads below a barrel-vaulted church ① to a confluence of two streams. Go across a slope next to the stream on the left and then downhill to

0.15

the larger stream again. A **well house** is located there and, above it, another hill chapel. Wander uphill to the left in

0.20

the steam bed until **markings** lead you uphill to the right. Later you cross the dry stream bed again and come to a

0.28

fork, where you head downhill to the right. A pump building is located directly after, on the left along the stream

0.30

bed. It is only a few steps from there up to the **street**.

0.35

Go up the street to the left and continue straight on. After the **ridge** (240 m above sea-level), go downhill until you reach the first curve. You will quickly discover the foot path leading steeply downwards. At the bottom, turn to the

0.45 right before the street and walk further downhill in the dry bed until you come to a **water passage** under the street.

0.55 After crossing over or under the street, you will see pines lining the way along the slate river bed ②. It is a wonderful path, even a **spring** is there. At the confluence with a stream coming down from the left, there is an old, water-

1.05 driven **grain mill** at the foot of the slope on the left. It hasn't ground grain for a long time. Water fell from the upright pipe into the building attached below, where the horizontal water wheel and above it the millstones were located. (Sketch on page 71)

1.10 Further down in the river bed, you come to a **road track** leading to the village of Diafáni. The new cement walls here were built to prevent another flood catastrophe like the one in October 1994.

One of the first buildings on the left is the boarding house "Munich". Nomen est omen. Instead of a view of the sea, you see the mountains. The wide cement canal leads to the village. You leave the river bed to the left in the old

1.25 section and continue straight on to the **jetty in Diafáni.** The inn-keepers know, however, how to prevent you from boarding the ship right away.

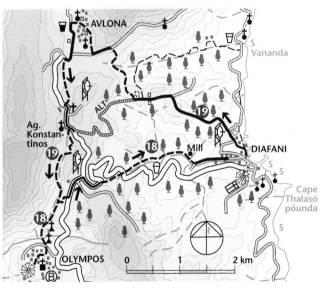

⑲ The Ascent to Ólympos

This four-hour walking tour shows Òlympos in harmony with the grand world of the mountains. The first sight of Ólympos will remain unforgettable. From Diafáni, you wander up along a forest path and an old calderími to the village of Avlóna, which seems removed from our times and where you can stop for some refreshment. From there, you walk uphill along one of the loveliest paths on the islands to the picturesque mountain village Ólympos. At AWT 0.50 you could begin an alternative circuit tour with a swim.

▶ See previous page for map.

AWT	
0.00	From the **boat jetty in Diafáni**, walk towards the north for a few metres, turn inland (to the left) at the baker's oven and continue uphill to the right at the taverna. At the next fork, bear uphill to the left along a dirt road out
0.08	of the village. At the **fork** in the road, bear to the right,
0.12	past antennas (left), until you come to the next **fork** in front of a round water tank.

Of course, you should take the narrower path leading uphill to the left through a sparse pine forest. The trees have been bent to the right by the wind as time has passed. Still fighting against it, bend your head and torso to the left.

0.40   Once you have reached the top, you come to a **fork**, where you go to the left and then stroll above a valley along almost level ground ①. Somewhat later you change to the other side of the hill and look down into the valley

on the right. After walking between the ruins of two
0.50 houses, you come to an **olive grove** enclosed by a wall on
the right.

>   *Short cut:* By staying on the dirt road, you avoid Avló-
>   nas and arrive directly at the church Ayios Konstan-
>   tinos.
>
>   *Alternative:* Still beneath the field, a very lovely, well-
>   marked path leads through pine forests and stream
>   beds to the **beach at Vanánda** in 35 minutes. For a
>   description, see ⑳ after AWT 3.15

0.50 *Above* the enclosed grove, the way you should go further
turns off to the right. It is a path from times long past,
covered with stones. It meanders pleasantly across the
1.05 plateau ②, traverses a hollow, goes past a **gate** and is inter-
rupted shortly after that by another dirt road. Walk along
it to the left for 200 m and then uphill to the right. On the
left, fields are embedded in the plateau. The village of
1.15 **Avlóna** is located behind the hill.

>   *Time seems to have stood still here – if only there weren't
>   any electric wires. Narrow paths nestle around the
>   houses; there are scattered old bucket wells and alónis,
>   the threshing areas. Everything still functions. This
>   "outer village" is only inhabited at harvest time. There is
>   now a taverna here, and you can look forward to drinks
>   from an electric refrigerator.*

From the taverna, continue to the south, toward the antennas, along the dirt road, which will soon be asphalted.
Friendly men and women in lovely old traditional cos-
tumes will wave to you from the fields. The dirt road as-
cends slowly and, in the first hair needle curve to the
right, you will find the familiar colour signals which our

predecessors put there to show us the old paths. Continue straight on across the bottom of the valley along the path

1.30 and then through a **gate** and up to the ridge. You meet up
1.40 with the street again there and quickly reach the **Church of Constantine** ③ by walking along it to the left. The church is situated magnificently in front of beautiful mountain scenery and at first still hides the splendid view of Ólympos.

Walk downhill along the street, and, about 30 m after the church, you will see the beginning of the old path, which runs parallel to the street in the beginning but later leads

★ steeply downhill. The view you enjoy here belongs to the most beautiful in the Aegean ④. Behind Ólympos steep cliffs rise up as in a dreamlike landscape. It is a sight that could also come from the Andes or the Himalayas.

Walk to the right at first, then to the left and later in the
2.10 **stream bed**. Beneath a chapel on the hill there is a well house – this is where you leave the stream bed to the
2.20 right. Beneath Ólympos **steps** lead up to a dirt road. Walk along it to the left at first and then to the right to the
2.30 **windmills of Ólympos**. The sea glitters on the other side of the mountain. By walking along the windmills, you reach the beautiful village. Since it has become evening in the meanwhile, it isn't so crowded any more.

▶ The taverna in **Avlóna** has new **rooms for guests** with traditional furnishings and soufás, the Carpathian beds on podiums. Waking up in this remote village is a very special experience (Tel. 22 40-510 46).

⑳ The Lost City

This seven-hour walking tour, probably the most impressive on Kárpathos, is especially beautiful in spring but it demands a certain amount of fitness! There are no great heights to overcome, but the length of the tour - more than 20 km - is exhausting. The only possibility to find refreshments and to spend the night is in Avlóna, and even here this isn't always the case (tel. 22450-51046). So you must carry everything you need along with you, including an electric torch. An elegant short-cut would be to have a boat fetch you in Vroukoúnda (details ㉑ or to return from Avlona by taxi.

If you take a taxi to the starting point, have the driver go directly up to the church of Ayios Konstantínos.

AWT 0.00   Jump agilely out of the bus at the **turn-off to Avlóna**, walk uphill to the right along the asphalt street and leave the beautiful mountain village of Ólympos behind you. When the electric wires approach the street on the left, you can select a foot path under the wires as a short-cut.

0.15   Soon you will reach the **church of Ayios Konstantínos**, which offers the loveliest view of Ólympos, and then continue along the street, later heading downhill. Opposite the gravel quarry, pass through a gate to reach the old mule track leading downhill to Avlóna, which you will soon see. It is a wonderful stroll, and later you turn right

0.35   onto the cement street to arrive at **Avlóna** ①. More about it see walk ⑲.

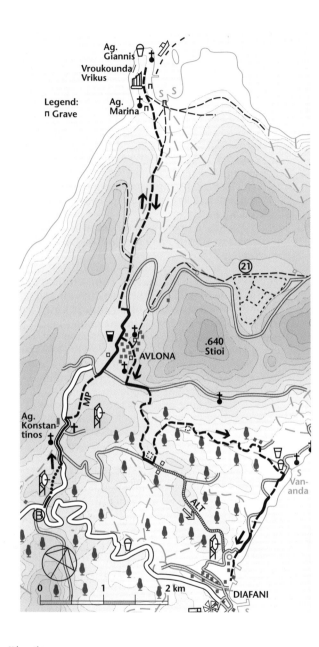

Ag.
Giannis

Vroukounda/
Vrikus

Legend:
π Grave

Ag.
Marina

21

.640
Stioi

AVLONA

MP

Ag.
Konstan-
tinos

ALT

S
Van-
anda

DIAFANI

0   1   2 km

You pass a village taverna on the main street and follow the wide dirt road for another five minutes, in several curves through fertile land, always following the signs for "Vroukounda" until you enter a portal of gigantic fig trees on the left ②.

0.50 The stone barriers along a monopáti lead to the sea, first slightly uphill, then to the right at a **fork**. The fields are no longer cultivated; the area becomes isolated. But the blue sea entices you downwards – partially on artistically constructed kalderímis, partially on gravel paths. The panorama extends from the sister island Saría on the right to the Vroukoúnda peninsula ③, situated like a table

1.20 mountain in front on the left. At the **fork**, you could follow the sign "Hohlackia" to the right and arrive at the beach, but it is easier to walk downhill to the left! The chapel Áyia Marína, into which the ancient building components have been fitted, is in front of the peninsula on the left between the cliffs.

You notice a massive boulder on the left of the main path, full of holes like a tooth with cavities and sheltering recesses for graves. Climb up the steps. On the left, the enormous square hewn stone walls of the ancient city arise, and beneath, on the right, there are more ancient graves which are not visible from here.

*The ancient **Dorian city of Vrikus** used to be located on the plateau. It was one of four Dorian cities on Kárpathos and Saría and was founded 3000 years ago. It is possible that a Mycenaean settlement was located in this easily defensible place even earlier. The city was still inhabited in Byzantine times but was then probably abandoned due to frequent attacks by pirates.*

Everything belongs to the past. Hardly any lanes or houses can be discerned, so many of the mid-high walls probably were used for agriculture.

1.40 Another interesting thing awaits you at the end of the peninsula: the underground **chapel of Ayios Giánnis**. The alter room is divided by two ancient pillars; from the ceiling, water drips into the marble cruciform baptismal font. The consecration of the church is on August 28. The atmosphere down here is indescribable when hundreds of candles are burning.

It is a long way back, so you should tank up on fresh water near the chapel and then quickly dive into the salt water. Behind the sandy-pebbly beach there are more grave chambers in the cliffs. These used to be closed by stone slabs. All of them are set up towards the sunrise. From the

2.50 beach, take the same way back to **Avlóna**.

> *Alternative:* If you want to go to Ólympos from here, use ⑲.

After the taverna, turn left into one of the lanes, walk uphill in a zigzag line and then turn to the right. At the southern end of the village, you will see the barrel-vaulted chapel of Ayios Nikolaos ④, which you pass before you

3.00 meet a **dirt road**. Follow the road about 150 paces to the left, where you will find markings on the right leading down to the old kalderími. It first leads through the hollow, then over a hilltop and down to a fragrant, shady pine forest.

3.15 Walk around a **walled-in olive grove** (left) and then 50 m downhill to the left along the wide forest path.

> *Short Cut:* If you stay on the wide forest path and disregard two turn-offs to the left, not walking downhill to the left until after the antennas of **Diafáni**, you can order something to drink from Vassilis in the "Chrissi Akti" 40 minutes later.

3.15 The more romantic way, however, turns off to the left below the walled-in olive grove. You walk downhill along slaty ground beneath pines. Cross through the bottom of

!! the valley and pay close attention to the directional arrows which have been carefully set up there. Head towards the sea on the left above the stream bed. Pass a

3.30 walled-in **olive grove** and later you will come to the stream bed again. Walk on the left above the stream bed for a while, then in it for several more minutes. When you

see a house on the left of the slope, leave the stream bed
towards the left and then turn uphill to the left again into
3.50 olive terraces shortly afterwards. After the **house** (left) at
the "Odos kanari", turn to the right into the stream bed
again and leave it to the right later to reach the **beach of**
3.55 **Vanánda**. There is a fountain and a kind of garden restaurant here.
Use the dirt road briefly on the way back and take three
lovely short-cuts to the left along the rocky cliff to short-
4.20 en the way to **Diafáni**.

The World of the Gods

At the beginning of all things, the Terra Mater, Gaia, the goddess
of the earth, appeared out of Chaos. In her sleep, she bore Uranos
out of herself and took him as her husband.

Kronos and his sister Rhea, as well as other Titans, resulted from
this unusual relationship. The two of them also united, upholding
the family's tradition, and parented the goddesses Hera (later
the Roman Juno, protector of the military aristocracy), Hertia (the
Roman Vesta, goddess of the domestic hearth) and Demeter
(Ceres, goddess of the fields) as well as the gods Zeus (Jupiter),
Poseidon (Neptune) and Hades (Pluto).

The men divided up the world among themselves: Zeus took
Olympus and thus domination; his brothers had the sea and the
underworld. Zeus, the highest of the gods, lord of heaven and
earth, also took his sister Demeter as his wife, who bore the gods
Ares (Mars, the Roman god of war), Eilythia, Hebe and Hephaistos
(Vulcan). From Zeus's relationships with 15 other godly sisters,
there resulted, among others, Artemis, Apollo, Hermes and
Aphrodite. Artemis (Roman Diana) is the goddess of the hunt;
Apollo represents right, order and peace; Hermes (Mercury) is the
protector of wanderers, shepherd, tradesmen and rogues, while
Aphrodite (Venus) is the goddess of sensual love and beauty.

Zeus was not just on the way in heaven. Meanwhile, there were
lovely princesses on earth, too. He approached them in various
forms, for example as a bull, swan and even as the husband of
one of the women he desired. Thus the Heroes Minos, Perseus,
Helena and Herakles, in addition to fifteen others, were born.
They were, however, only half-gods, representing the link between heaven and earth.

㉑ All Alone

If you want to do a walking tour all by yourself, you should take along a mobile phone since you might not meet anyone who could help you for hours. This also means that, except for swimming suits, everything you need must be carried with you along the way. There is water at the beginning and at the end of the tour.

Walking the stretch in both directions (each 10 km), which takes four hours in each direction, is recommended only as fitness training. The tour is commendable not only because of the landscape but especially because of the beautiful old paths. It is advisable to do one leg by boat. You can find tips concerning this at the end of the description. For overnight accommodations, see page 87

Both directions are described in detail here.

AWT **Avlóna – Trístomo**

The most comfortable way to start the tour is in **Avlóna**. (Indefatigable walkers can also get there by ⑱ instead of taking a taxi or hitching a ride). From the **taverna**, walk along the road 30 m to the north towards the end of the village, then to the right at the sign and to the left at the cross street. Blue dots lead out of the village along a monopáti. There is also a large sign towards Trístomo there. After a gate, the lane becomes a foot path which crosses a dirt road shortly afterwards. The wide stone walk proceeds uphill on the right of the slope. The walled-in fields in the valley are the island's granary. Many of the

0.00

0.07

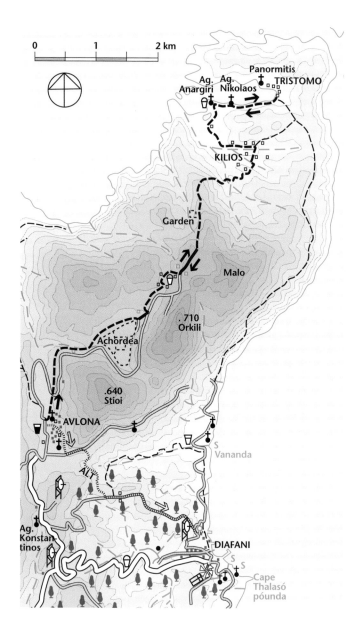

inhabitants of Olympos and Diafáni have fields here. Avlóna is an "exterior village" and is not inhabited year round.

0.15 After a **gate**, turn your back to the valley. Soon there is a
water pump on the right and in front of you is the fertile
valley of Achórdea ①. Before the walls around the fields, a

0.25 **sign** directs you to the left, always staying next to the
wall. A water hose accompanies you.

0.40 At the end of the walls, there is another **pump**. From
there, follow the dirt road for five minutes, then turn left

0.45 at a large **boulder** marked in blue and follow the foot
path which runs parallel to the dirt road. Between the
walls and the remains of some buildings, you come to a

1.00 **cistern** and shortly afterwards, between two pumps, to a
1.05 dirt road which you follow to its **end**.

On the left, a marked path leads downhill and then above
a garden. Walk along a wonderful stone path part of the
time, more or less downhill, until you can see the plains
of Kilios ② and the island of Saría from the last hill. From
the summit, the carefully laid flagstone path zigzags
down to the fertile plains. They were cultivated until the
1970s.

At the bottom, cross over the first dry stream bed with a
short turn to the left and then turn downhill to the left in
the second. Near the sea, the field walls are left behind,
the pond is on the left and, over a small hill, you arrive at

2.00 the **chapel of Ay. Anargíri**. Here you can have a rest at a
cistern. On the southern side of the bay, you pass the

2.15 Nicholas chapel on the way to **Trístomo**.

Two old people still live here; the others have moved
away and left behind empty buildings. A lonely place.

Trístomo – Avlóna
If you walk both ways, use the 2nd time indicated.

0.00= From abandoned **Tristomo**, walk directly along the water
2.15 to the Nicholas chapel with its boat pier ③ and then on to

0.15/ the chapel of **Ay. Anargíri**. If you want to swim, this is
2.30 the easiest place to get into the water.

From the chapel, walk over the small hill, then on the left
of the pond and, after a ruin, continue around the field
walls in a curve to the right ④ until you come to the **ruins**

0.20/ **of a house**, where you go uphill slightly. The blue mark-
2.35 ings found here later lead you downhill to a place where
two arid valleys meet. Follow the left one uphill, with the

ruins of the houses in the abandoned village Kilios on the
0.40/ left, then later a big **fig tree** on the right, where you con-
2.55 tinue to the right. Two minutes later, cross a dry stream
bed diagonally off towards the left (arrows) and cheerfully
begin the ascent. Soon you come to a large boulder next
to a house. The zigzag path with steps used to be the only
1.05/ connection to Ólympos by land. The ascent to the **first**
3.20 **hill top** at 285 m above sea-level costs the most energy. In
exchange, you can enjoy the view of Saría. A less steep
1.20/ stretch follows to the next **pass** (380 m above sea-level).
3.35 From here, you can see a deserted, walled-in garden and,
behind it, the beginning of a wider path. You reach this
1.30/ **dirt road** after an easy ascent. Walk uphill along the dirt
3.45 road and across the hill top until it forks at two **water**
1.35/ **pumps** near some walls.
3.50 Go to the right here, then immediately to the left, past a
cistern, and on to the right near the walls. At 430 m above
sea-level, you have reached the zenith of this tour. Now
descend between walls towards the Achórdea plains.
2.50/ At a **boulder** with blue markings, change to the left onto
4.05 the dirt road leading downhill. It forks at a pump – go on
the right of the walls along the water hose. At the end of
3.10/ the walls, turn right at the **sign** (left) and walk uphill
4.25 along a wide flagstone path. There is a deep gorge cut in
3.15/ below you on the right; later, another **water pump** is on
4.30 the left.
Fields appear in front of you. After a gate, walk to the left,
and soon you can see Avlóna with its antennas. Cross
over the dirt road which has accompanied you invisibly
3.35/ up higher for so long to reach the "outside village" of
4.50 **Avlóna**, which is only inhabited at harvest time. You can

get something to eat and drink here and could have a taxi fetch you. Or you can spend the night here!

If you want to wander **to Diafáni**, follow ⑳, but take the alternative along the forest path as a short-cut at the walled-in olive grove (AWT 3.15). This takes an hour.

⑲ leads **to Ólympos** beginning at AWT 1.15.

▶ The taverna in **Avlóna** has new **rooms for guests** with traditional furnishings and soufás, the Carpathian beds on podiums. Waking up in this remote village is a very special experience (Tel. 22 40-510 46).

▶ Nikos Orphános, captain and owner of a lovely hotel, can take wanderers **to Trístomos by boat** or fetch them. Sharing a boat with others is more reasonable. His office is at the harbour, tel. 224 50-512 89.

▶ For **individual wanderers**, there is sometimes a cheaper possibility: if you contact the captain of the **excursion boat** "Karpathos ll" a day in advance, you can arrange to be let off in Trístomos. The disadvantage is that you won't arrive there until 11.15 and will have to wander in the heat of the day.

㉒ Saría

This small walk around the island takes two and a half hours and can easily be done during a day's excursion to this neighbouring island since the boat stays here for about three and a half hours. You must take along drinks and something to eat. Part of the way leads downhill through boulders without a path, but it is not very steep.

AWT 0.00 — Get off the boat in **Palátia** and walk uphill beneath the tamarisk trees along the stream bed. After a few metres, the hidden chapel of Sophia becomes visible on the left. From the 6th century on, a much larger church was located here, allegedly with 101 doors. The remains of its walls can still be seen. Even much earlier, in Doric times, a city existed here.

Follow the blue arrows leading to a narrow gorge. The walls of the cliff rise almost vertically on the right and the

0.20 — left. A plateau extends behind the gorge, and the **path forks** here. The path to the left leads to the southern point of the island. If you walk there, you need a boat to pick you up. See below.

Continue uphill on the right to the dilapidated **village of Argos**, which has been abandoned for about 25 years. There are fountains in front of a few houses, and you can still find water in them. Some of the houses are even furnished. Their owners come from Diafáni to look after the goats at certain intervals.

After walking through the village, turn to the right towards one fig tree standing all alone. Walk around it and

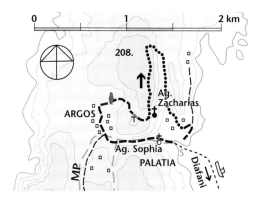

then, staying on the right, wander up the hill. You pass a

0.35 **cross** at the top and then see the white **church of Ay. Zacharias** ①. The former inhabitants of Argos and their descendants meet here for the consecration of the church every year on September 5. For wanderers, too, it is a very lovely spot to have a rest.

Then walk along the edge of the steep slope without a path towards the north. About 300 m after the highest el-

0.50 evation, there is the best place **to descend** to the high valley located on the right – without a path and even on the seat of your breeches at times. Stay on the right to reach

1.00 the **middle of the valley** and continue on the right to the south to come to the way out of the plateau again. A long time ago this area was cultivated. Walls along the fields testify to this. It must have been terribly laborious - stones, nothing but stones.

1.15 At the end of the level area, you come to **ruins of houses** and circle the hill to the left. Large circular remains of houses, similar to bee hives, rise up there, the "palaces" ②. They have given the bay the name "Ta Palátia" and are said to have been built by Syrian pirates 600 years ago. In the lower valley connecting to here, follow an old mule

1.25 track down to the **bay**. You can frolic in the clear water until the ship leaves again.

▶ Captain *Nikos Orphanos* offers boat connections between Diafáni and Saría for **combination boat and walking tours**. His office is directly at the pier in Diafáni, tel. 224 50-512 89.

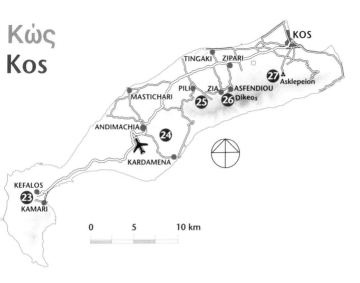

Κὼς
Kos

The home of Hippocrates is the Greek island which is most characterised by tourism. The elegant holiday and spa guests of the olden days have now been replaced by all-inclusive tourists attracted by the beautiful beaches. Hotels and tourist establishments border the sea.

In addition, the city of Kos is well worth visiting, with its interesting buildings from the past 2000 years. It is a very special kind of open air museum.

Kos is not necessarily an island for walking tours. Large parts of it are flat, are closely built with houses and can be discovered more easily on a rental bicycle.

The hilly peninsula of Kéfalos and the Dikéos massif are topographically more interesting and better suited for wandering. The effective public bus system makes these areas easy to reach.

The Dikéos Mountains form the backbone of the elongated island. In the south it rises steeply from the sea; to the north, it comes to a gentle end in the water. In the mountains, where you can walk in shady pine forests, you can find springs all year long.

Day excursions with walking tours on Níssiros and Psérimos are possible from Kos.

㉓ Above the Sheep's Head

Seen from the air, the western end of Kos looks like a sheep's head - which is probably the reason for the Greek name "Kéfalos" – "head". This rather strenuous walking tour takes three hours one way and leads from Kamári across the high ridge to the wildly romantic coast of Kata - and ends at a good taverna. Along the way you come to the idyllic ruins of a church and a dilapidated amphitheatre. If you want to enjoy a wonderful sunset over the sea, you should have a taxi fetch you from the taverna "Theológos" (224 20-714 28 or -715 96).

The tour can also be begun in the country village of Kéfalos and be made 15 minutes shorter.

AWT   If you set out in **Kéfalos**, you need 15 minutes from the beginning of the village on the street to the south, past the cemetery and the sports area to the church of Panagía Palatianí. It is located on an elevation on the left of the street (= AWT 0.30).

0.00   From the **harbour in Kamári**, walk inland at the recommendable restaurant "Fáros" and turn left at the second

0.08   **turn-off**, shortly before the street goes uphill. *Before* the big sandy grounds, stay on the right and walk to the right in front of the sandstone slope ① into the valley until the path ends at a field. Continue to the right without a path and then walk up a wide slope on the left along the incline.

From here, cross over several stone walls (red dots) on the

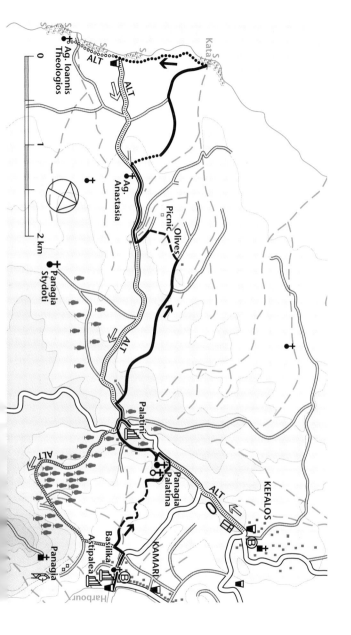

Ag. Ioannis
Theologios

ALT

Ag.
Anastasia

Picnic

Olives

Panagia
Stydoti

Kata

ALT

ALT

0

1

2 km

ALT

Palatini

Panagia
Palatina

ALT

KEFALOS

Basilika
Astipalea

KAMARI

Panagia

Harbour

B

terraces to reach a foot path, which then turns into a dirt road. It ends at the street beneath the church of **Panagía**

0.30 **Palatianí**.

> *The upper chapel with the blue barrel-vaulted roof is the successor of the lower one, which is now a church in ruins ②, with ancient architectural components everywhere in its walls. These "spoils" come from the temple to Dionysos which was originally located here. The builders of the ancient temple picked out a wonderful place, as they did so often.*

Return the way you came but, several metres before you reach the street, turn left onto the dirt road. Don't let the artistic scarecrows frighten you. Pass by two farmhouses and bear right uphill at the fork through a farmyard whose chaotic disorder will surely cause some surprise for most people. Barking dogs in a cage complete the picture.

0.40 Walk along the **street** on the right, then straight on 100 m past the crossing to find a fence with an entry on the right.

> *On the right above the entry, you can find traces of the pedestal and barrels of some pillars from a temple to Demeter. A statue now exhibited in the archaeological museum in Kos was excavated here.*
>
> *Further down, round steps used as seats have been built harmoniously into the slope. These are the remains of the Hellenistic **amphitheatre of Palátia**, dating back to the 2nd century BC. The lovely view of the bay enjoyed by the early theatre-goers is now unfortunately almost completely overgrown.*

Back at the crossing once again, walk along the street to the right now and turn off it to the right after about

100 m. Pass the farmstead on the left while you stroll into a gentle landscape ③ with a phalanx of wind rotors from our modern world rotating above it. Individual pumice-stone boulders tower up from the agricultural valley. At

0.55 the fork, bear left until you come to a **house** standing alone in a field on the right. Opposite it, a dirt road turns off to the left. Wander downhill along it on the left edge of an olive grove until you reach a field of grain with a path on its lower side. The path goes through a hollow and then crosses a dirt road, which you should take up-hill to the left. (Going to the right takes you to a lovely picnic spot next to the ruins of a house, with a view over the wide coastal landscape.)

1.05 At the top, turn right at the **street** and jog downhill on
1.20 the asphalt to the **chapel of Anastásia**. Follow a path on the opposite side of the street to a hill for a short while and work your way down through the bushes on the oth-
1.25 er side to get to the fertile **coastal plains**. A dirt road on the opposite side of the field of grain meanders to the left through a beautiful heather landscape. At the fork, bear
1.45 right to get to the beach at **Káta**.

Wind and sea have carved fantastic forms into the chalk cliffs. There is finer sand in the northern area.

Walk above the cliffs ④ to the south between heather
2.05 shrubs to arrive at Ayios Ioánnis Theológos – the **taverna**.
OW (The chapel on the beach which is further to the south and has the same name does not necessarily belong to the compulsory programme of things you must see on Kos.) Enjoy a nice breather on the terrace and let yourself be spoiled by the friendly waiters. In contrast to those who have come by car, you have really earned this break!

The way back: You reach the ridge on foot along the street in 50 minutes and need another 30 minutes down to Kamári. Up on the ridge, you can go right at the cross-ing and then take the second dirt road downhill to the left (see map).

It is, however, more pleasant to enjoy the sunset in the taverna and return by taxi or to get a ride with the nice people sitting at the table next to yours.

㉔ The Crusaders' Fortress

This two-and-a-half to three-hour circular tour presents typical valleys eroded in the sandstone characteristic of the western half of Kos. Starting at the sea, you wander to the gigantic citadel of Antimáchia, which dominates the valley of Kardámena.

AWT

0.00

0.10

0.35

The point of departure is the cemetery (Greek: "tafos") in **Kardámena**. You reach it by walking out of the city to the north-east along the street "Odos Dodekanisou". Soon you will see the cemetery's church with its greenish barrel-vaulted roof in the fields. From the **cemetery**, walk along the street to the north-west towards the hills. Above the plains, the gigantic, expansive fortress stands guard. On the left of the walls, the builders dug out a trough to keep attackers at a distance.

Pay no regard to the turn-off to the left, and soon you will come to a very high warehouse on the left of the street. About 200 m after it, you won't believe your eyes: a new **monopáti**, turning off uphill to the right, has been built here for tourists. Walk upwards in serpentines ① above a wide hollow eroded into the stone with an enormous olive grove embedded in it. On the horizon, you can see the volcanic island of Níssiros. The footpath leads almost to the **citadel's** artificial trench ②.

Kos belonged to Venice from 1204 on, and it was the Venetians who built this fortress. After 1309, it was enlarged and fortified by its next masters, the Order of Saint John. After the fall of Rhodes in 1523, an honourable withdrawal from Kos was granted to the Order, and the citadel was

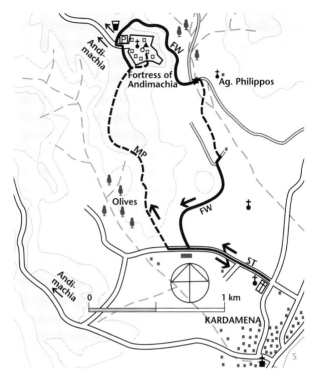

handed over to the Turks. Only the bulwark walls of the fortress are still standing; the buildings within them are all in ruins. The two chapels date from more recent times.

Due to renovations, the main entrance in the round bastion is closed at the moment. On the side towards the sea, however, the fortress can be "taken by storm".

A place to eat is 300 m away on the street.

From the parking area, walk downhill on the other side into a valley eroded into the stone. Down in the plains, follow a dirt road coming from the left towards the right

0.50 for a short while and, after the **bridge**, walk to the right again onto a tractor track. Accompanied by a water pipe, it leads to a farmstead. Leave the farm on your left and

1.00 take the **dirt road** to the right, following its winding way

1.10 until you arrive at the street with the high **warehouse**

1.20 again. To the left, the street leads back to the **cemetery**.

㉕ The Turtles in Paléo Pilí

If you don't meet up with a turtle on this 3¹/₂-hour walking tour, then you haven't paid attention. Many of these slow animals are at home on the plateau. You walk a bit more quickly, climb up the ruins of a castle and arrive at the ghost town of Paléo Pilí. This easy tour is seven kilometres long and surmounts 250 metres in altitude. There are a few places to eat in Amanioú and two springs along the way.

AWT When you have arrived in the upper section of **Pilí** (Ay. Nikolaos) by bus, you can fill your water bottle at the 500-
0.00 year-old village fountain. From the **platía**, the village square in this town which has retained its quaintness very well, walk uphill along the street. After 200 m, follow the
0.04 **sign** to the "Heroon of Charmylos" to the left, but walk straight on at the second sign.

*On the left, there is the so-called **grave of Harmylos**, a mythological hero. The sober barrel vaults, each with six lateral recesses for graves, were built upon many times, the last time with a chapel whose walls contain ancient building components from the former constructions*

Before the fork further down along the road, walk to the right into an olive grove and then uphill along its left
0.10 edge. After the **gully** in the ground, walk uphill on a footpath to a wide dirt road, which you should follow steeply upwards to the right. From the round hilltop, you can see the ruins of a house on the next hill – the next goal. Down on the left, there is a military depot, which ex-

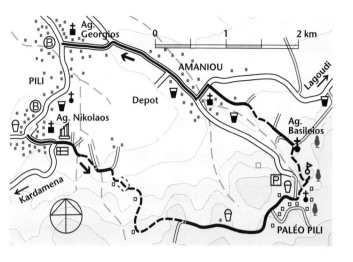

plains why the spot is not suitable for taking holiday photos.

0.20 Down in the hollow, leave the dirt road at the oleander plants by walking to the right through a small **gate** and then following a narrow path up to the ruins of the house. Behind it, there is a flat field with a passageway (red dot) through the wall at the right of its back end. This is where a footpath lined with bushes and kermes oaks begins to lead uphill to the next ruins. Pass by these on the left, then walk on the left of the wall through rocky ter-

0.40 rain to arrive at the third set of **ruins**, 50 m away on the right side of the path, which now makes a wide curve to the left ①. Soon you will find a convenient goat path. Up above on the right, the chapel of Saint George reveals itself briefly in a groove in the terrain. In the sea, you can see Kálymnos and, on the right of it, Psérimos. Along the coast of Kos, there is the former salt-pit, which is now a bird sanctuary. As so often, the mountain with the antennas is dedicated to the prophet Elijah.

0.45 At the top, you meet up with a **dirt road**, which you follow to the left. Past a farmstead and (probably) a few turtles, you come to a watering-place. The ruins of the old castle can already be seen ②.

First, go downhill through the remains of the village of

1.15   **Paléo Pilí** (Old-Pilí). The hidden location in the mountains protected the inhabitants from pirates, but not from illness. In 1830 the village was abandoned due to cholera. As you climb up through the remains of the walls, you pass a chapel to Mary with neglected frescoes.

1.25   Then you can enjoy the panorama of the northern coast from the **castle ruins**. The castle was constructed in the Byzantine period in the 12th century.

!!   As you walk back down, leave the path to the right *50 m before* the parking area to reach a lovely old paved path to

1.35   the **chapel of Ay. Basileios**. A dirt road opposite the shady sitting area leads downhill. At the fork, go left to a gate and through it to the old footpath to the church on the left. Pass by the second gate on the right since the old path is too overgrown from here on. Later, stay on the left of the footpath to reach the street along a dirt road. Go

1.55   left to **Amanioú**. Here you can refresh yourself for the last lap. You cannot walk straight on across the terrain since it is a restricted military area. Instead, take the street back to

2.10   **Pilí** (lower section of town Ay. Geórgios).

㉖ The Peak

This three-hour ascent to the peak is a must, even for languid holiday bathers. It should be undertaken on a clear day since sudden fog can become a problem. Don't forget water!
The moderately steep ascent of 550 metres in altitude is very well marked with red arrows and leads through pine forests. Those afraid of heights needn't have any second thoughts – only one short passage beneath the peak could be problematic.

AWT   The little village of **Zía**, located in a lovely spot in a mountain forest, is a disappointment for the new-comer at first since there are rows of shops lined up next to one another. In the upper section, however, there are nice houses and small streets. Walk up the lane beginning di-

0.00   rectly on the right of the **bus stop**, leaving the shops and stands behind you after a few metres. You come to a water mill (left) and walk across the terrace of an eating place to reach the church up above. Turn right here, then bear right again at the fork and follow the "Way to the Mountain". The time indication showing two hours and twenty minutes doesn't seem to come from a mountaineering club. Blue dots accompany you up the cement street. Af-

0.10   ter a house (right), turn right onto a **sandy street**, where you will soon enjoy the pleasant shade from pine trees. 50

0.15   m after a chapel ①, go through a **gate** on the left. Walk uphill behind the fence, staying on the right. The peak can't be seen yet. You meet up with the sandy street again after walking up the lovely old rocky path. Walk upwards

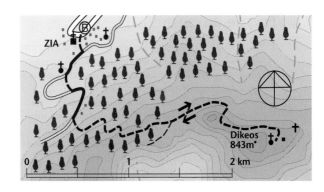

0.20   to the left on the street and soon you will see a small **farm**
        house (left). After another house, walk for 200 m enjoy-
0.25   ing the pine aroma until a red **metal arrow** on the left in-
        dicates the beginning of the ascent through the woods.
0.45   Bear **left** at a fork to reach a **lower mountain** after a
0.55   curve to the right. From here you have a view of the other
        side of the island and the old fishing harbour of Kardáme-
        na, which has surrendered quite thoroughly to tourism.
        Follow red dots and arrows to a ridge. With your destina-
        tion in sight, walk downhill at first and then up to the
1.10   chapel at the **peak** ②. You can look out over the gentle
OW   north side and the rugged southern coast of Kos, sur-
        rounded by many of the Dodecanese islands and the nar-
        row Turkish peninsula of Resadiye. You will gladly light a
        candle at the peak for this view. The inhabitants of Kos
        love to celebrate up here. A xenonas, an empty refuge, of-
        fers the possibility of staying the night and having protec-
        tion from bad weather.

㉗ To the Asklepieion

If you haven't overburdened yourself at the souvenir shops in Zía, you can wander down the approximately eight kilometres to the famous excavations of the Asklepieion along a wide panoramic path in three to four hours. You pass through two abandoned villages but will find no fountains.

AWT
0.00

At the end of Zía's shopping mile, walk past the **taverna "Ayli"**, heading out of the village. Pass the bus parking area on the left and turn off to the right onto a wide dirt road. After 150 m, wander down into the woods on the left until you come to a small stone

0.08

bridge, where you take the foot path to **Athómatos**, a section of the village of Asfendíou. It is decaying and has almost been abandoned by the locals – it is easier to earn money on the coast. Individual houses are being restored by foreigners. On the left of the church to Saint George ①, you come to some well-tread steps leading uphill and, staying slightly on the right, arrive at the sandy track again.

0.25
!!

Walk along the flat track to the left and enjoy the lovely view with olive groves and the sea. At the **fork**, take the upper path leading straight on but then, after about eight minutes, you must be careful not to miss the **footpath** *leading downhill to the left*. It is marked with a red dot and becomes narrow further down due to a large boulder. After passing through another

0.35

abandoned hamlet, you come to the **church of Ay. Dimitrios** ②. One family still lives here – the others

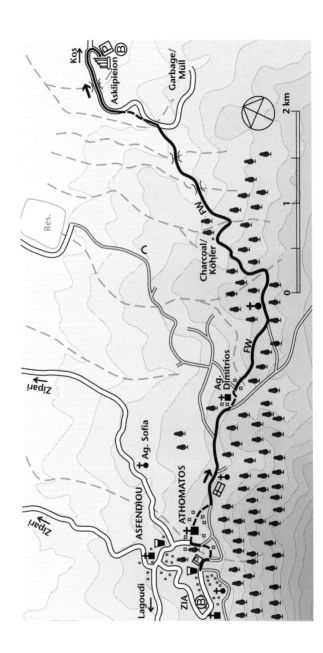

have left. You can look into the lovely interior of the church from the anteroom, and from the vestibule you see the harmonious landscape.

0.55　Ascending slightly, the wider dirt road (right) returns to the track, passing a chapel (left) and, after several curves, arriving at a house (left) with a magnificent view of the countryside and sea. A **charcoal-burner** lives and works here. The usual conception of charcoal-burners living deep in the woods is not valid here. This charcoal-burner swears that the best wood comes from olive trees and has thus chosen the ideal spot. In addition, he enjoys a lovely view while the wood glows slowly for seven days.

1.25　The rest of the way winds down to the **street** along eroded gullies. Up on the right, there is the rubbish pit. Walk downhill to the left through sprawling settlements as quickly as possible, sometimes taking short-cuts between the serpentine curves. After a
1.45　**bridge**, walk along flat land until you reach the
2.00　**Asklepieion**.

This "sanatorium" was dedicated to Asklepios (in Latin: Aesculapius), Apollo's son and the god of medicine and healing. More than 300 shrines to Asklepios are said to have existed; this was the most important one. Even the location is magnificent, although the view of the mainland is now almost completely overgrown. It was constructed between the 3rd century BC and the late ancient times and then expanded in the Hellenistic and Roman periods. The site was dominated in an exciting crescendo by a temple on the highest of the three levels of terraces. The altar, the oldest building, was located on the middle level, with porticoes forming the reception on the lowest level. After its destruction by an earthquake, the sanctuary was forgotten and wasn't excavated by the German archaeologist Rudolf Herzog until 100 years ago.

From here, there is a little trolley-train back to town.

Chálki

The entry into the harbour offers one of the most beautiful scenes in all of Greece. The respectable merchants' houses have been restored with loving care and offer lodging for visitors. They are preferably leased directly to guests from the UK. The island counts on a more distinguished and quieter kind of mature tourist. There are very few private accommodations. You are well taken care of in the hotel "Chálki" at the harbour, a lovely hotel constructed out of remodelled Italian barracks. You can purchase a copy of the pre-war Italian map of the island for walking tours. It is topographically exact but doesn't indicate any new streets. The former monopátia shown can often hardly be found any more.

㉘ The Green Side

The harsh landscape above the picturesque village of Nimbório hardly lets you suspect that the island also has green areas. Some of them will be discovered on this tour – in a side valley and also on the island's exterior side.
To get there, you need two hours time, a bottle of water and, according to your wishes, food and swim gear.

AWT   The tower of the church of Saint Nicholas, the highest on
       the Dodecanese, arises on the north side of the harbour of
0.00   **Nimbório**. At the **rear exit of the churchyard** with its

wonderful pebble surface, hop sprightly up the three steps, walk to the right along the lane and then bear left at the fork. Pass the pension "Captain's House" and cross the street. Up at the edge of the village you can later see dilapidated houses, which you can reach along small detours.

On the right of these houses, a gate reveals a monopáti leading uphill on the left of a wall into stony nature. After a right curve, head towards the ruins of a chapel, but turn off uphill to the left 250 m before them, where the wall ends on the right. A mid-high cistern is on the left here.

0.10
0.15 Cross over a **hill** to walk down through an olive grove and arrive at a **cement street** behind it.

Walk comfortably downhill along the street for 300 m until just before a thick pine forest. Open the double gate on the left of the street skilfully and follow the dirt road, with the trees on your right. As you walk, look for a cave up on the slope. In a left curve, leave the road to the right, climb uphill over stone terraces, always towards the cave, under which you must walk through a queer passageway made of bed-spring frame and walk to the right.

For a few metres the way is almost flat, and then you go uphill to the left into the rocks along a narrow marked
0.40 path. Up on the **ridge**, there are abandoned fields whose cultivation hasn't been worthwhile for a long time now. As you continue your way, you are suddenly in between juniper bushes. This lovely green region is called "Pefkia", which means pines. There aren't many of them left, however, although it rains more often up here ①.

Return by the same path, but turn off downhill to the left *before the cave*. Then you must imitate the goats and de-

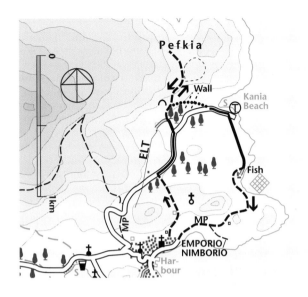

scend across the terraces in the fields to the street and the
1.05 **beach at Kaniá**. "Beach" is a bit exaggerated, of course,
but it is sufficient for a swim.

25 m before the petrol station for fishermen, walk along a
field track to the right at the edge of the sea to arrive at
1.10 the **fish hatchery** ②.

> *When almost all the fish in the Mediterranean had been
> caught, the appetite for fish grew even greater. Here you
> can see a solution to the problem: fish spawn along with
> food is brought over from Italy, fed to become breams and
> is then, for the most part, sent back again.*

About 40 m before the hall, take a footpath to the right,
circle the installation and then walk along the seaside for
a little bit again. After a mid-high cliff, turn uphill to the
right and cross over a water hose to come to a narrow
path up to a hill. First of all, you should enjoy the beautiful panorama view of the harbour there, with the Kastro
1.35 Mountain up above. You are back in **Nimbório** quickly
again and can look for a nice table at the harbour. Read
the menu with special interest today. Is bream on it?

㉙ Faded Frescoes

The famous high monopáti leading to the cloister of Ayios Ioánnou has unfortunately been expanded to become a sandy street. A variation on parallel paths is described here. Food and water must be carried along. You can see ancient chapels, faded frescoes, two abandoned villages and the ruins of a castle.

AWT
0.00 At the pier in Nimbório, walk up the street, past the school and then along the "Blvd. Tarpon Spring" (a place in Florida which many sponge-divers emigrated to) to the
0.10 beach of **Póndamos**. After it, the street mounts and demands a certain amount of energy. Nick's island taxi will pass you several times as it takes guests up the hill. Don't show any weakness now!

The first destinations are in front of you: up on the left, the castle, and then the cloister of Taxiárchis amidst gardens on the mountain on the right. On the left of the way, there is a chapel and then a roadside cross. 100 m after this cross, open the gate up on the left and follow the old path uphill. It ends at a doorway in one of the street's curves. Follow the street for two curves until you find a footpath leading uphill on the left which will serve as a short-cut to
0.40 **Chorió**. This place was deserted after the war, but recently some houses have been restored by Greeks living abroad. If you want to enjoy the magnificent view from the ruins of the castle, first walk up to the larger church, then go through the door on the right in the churchyard and walk up to the left along the steep path. Opposite the entry to a

small barrel-vaulted chapel halfway up, you can clearly recognise the square hewn stones of a huge wall. They come from the Hellenistic acropolis which dominated the hill before the Order of Saint John arrived. The chapel to Mary is also ancient (890 AD, restored in 1971) and has frescoes inside.

0.55 You enter the **castle** of the Order of St. John (14th century) through the tower keep, the first section, enclosed on all sides and easily defensible. Completely unprotected frescoes await a better future in the castle's church. The most rewarding thing about the castle, however, is the vast view across the sea.

1.05 When you are back down on the **street**, take the old path on the left of the cemetery walls (with ancient components built in), through a gate and then uphill beneath the street until – along the street again – you come to an

1.15 interesting grotto **chapel** in the saddle. Directly after it, a cement way on the right leads down to the church of **Ayios Leftérios**. Behind the larger, white church, you can find a hidden ancient little church with old images whose faces were probably disfigured with scratches in the Islamic period. In order to prevent complete ruin, they have at least been protected by gauze.

Beneath the two churches, an old monopáti meanders towards the cloister of Taxiarchis, first through a hollow and then slightly uphill again. Walk uphill beneath the cloister without a path to reach the cloister gardens with

1.30 olive and mulberry trees and then **Moni Taxiárchis**, the cloister of the archangels, called "San Angela" in the Italian period. Here, too, the most interesting church is the smaller one with its frescoes. But the epicure on this side of eternity enjoys the wonderful picnic spot ⊡ up here and the view over to Rhodes most of all.

When you have enjoyed all this, wander along the flat

1.40 dirt road towards the west until you come to the **sandy street** and take two turns uphill to the right there. The slowly mounting street is a bit discouraging, but you are rewarded for your efforts with the view into the pleasant plateau with its fields enclosed by stone walls.

2.00 Along the dirt street, you come to the **torso of a windmill** and a small field chapel on the ridge on the right beneath Profitis Elias. The wide dirt road would lead to the cloister of Agios Ioánnou.

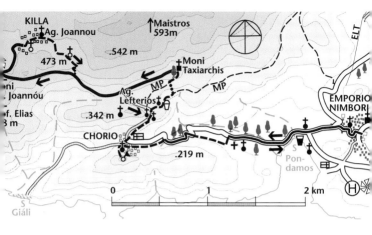

But you should take the way to the right leading to the abandoned settlement of **Kílla**. It is of Hellenistic origin and was an outside village for the goatherds from Chorió, abandoned after the Turkish period. Here, too, the remains of square hewn stones can be found in the ruins of the church and the remains of frescoes in the apse. As you walk around between the ruins with the wind whistling in your ears, you are quickly seized by an emotion of the finitude of mortal life, increased even more by the putrid smell from the dragon arum blossoms. Unfortunately, the

2.10   more recent church, **Ayios Ioánniou** ②, located on a dreamlike terrace, is locked shut.

Go back through the hollow in the south-east, behind which you can see the sea. If you expect to see more faded frescoes in the next chapel along the way, you will be disappointed – only the goats you disturb will jump out. The old path to the sea is easier to find from up above, and

2.25   you will soon come back to the **sandy street** below. Walk
3.10   to the left along it, past Chorió, to the beach of **Póndamos**. There are only two possibilities here: swimming or Nick's taverna.

▶ In addition to the hotel "Chálki" (tel. 22460-45208), the "Captain's House" (tel. 22460-45201) and the "Kleánthi" (tel. 22460-45334) offer possibilities for an **overnight stay**.

Kássos

Although Kássos is only four kilometres from Kárpathos, it is rarely frequented by foreign visitors. The sterile, over-sized harbour gives no reason to expect an idyllic island. This aspect can rather be found in the neighbouring old fishing harbour and the former anchoring area in Emborió. In addition, you will meet especially friendly people living in the island, and they will soon make you feel at home.

The landscape is almost devoid of trees and fairly barren. For walking tours, however, some monopátia and narrow dirt roads can still be discovered. The wind is extremely strong in the mountains and almost takes your breath away at times.

㉚ An Isolated Chapel along the Sea

This easy circular tour takes four hours and leads to an ancient shrine in a cave and to the vast northern coast with a chapel on the beach. You can only get refreshments in the villages.

AWT
0.00
From the small, picturesque **fishing harbour Fry** (see above), take the street leading uphill into the village, with the city hall and antenna on your right, and turn off to the right onto the next street. Walk respectfully on the right of the two white gentlemen and on up the right road. At the narrow street's turn-off to the right, continue straight on along the old footpath leading uphill along-

0.10
side the **cemetery**. Later a narrow lane passes on the right of a church and leads into the village of **Agía Marína**.

0.20 Continue uphill to arrive at the **outdoor café** at the top (still before the next large church) and walk along the larger street downhill to the left. Circle around an olive grove (left) in a wide left curve to come to a nicely restored windmill (left). At the traffic sign shortly after it,

0.30 walk to the right. Soon you will arrive at the **Fanoúrius Church** on the right with the torso of a windmill opposite it.

Afterwards, walk downhill slightly and then bear left/straight on at the fork. The cement comes to an end, and you continue straight on along the sand, with the sea on the right and two paths in front of you ①. The path on the left leads uphill to the cave (white arrow) and the one further right to the sea (blue arrow).

But first go *to the left* through a gate and then upwards between two new field walls. Beyond the sharp turn in the right wall, you can see the entrance to the cave ②. To get there, you must climb *over the wall on the right in front of a gate*.

0.45 *The Dorians closed the* **cave of Ellinikokamára** *with enormous square hewn stones on the side towards the sea. Before that, it had served as a site for worship and a hiding-place.*

If you don't want to climb down directly over the terrain walls from here, take the same way back and then go sharply to the left at the bottom.

0.55 A narrow cart track leads to a **goat pen** in a gully in the terrain, where you pass a gate. The way becomes a path

1.00 which soon leads past a **grotto chapel** (right). This subterranean room is also very impressive, in spite of being much smaller than the cave.

Cross another gorge, and you will find walls on the right lining the goat path. At the next gorge, you can see two 1.10 small **pump houses** on the opposite side as well as the end of the electric wires.

From here on, there is another dirt road leading slightly downhill. You can enjoy the vast view of the coast, watched over by a chapel ③. After a gate, meander down 1.25 to the **sea** along serpentine curves. There are wide pebble beaches here, and you have really earned them.

> *The **monument** at the parking area commemorates the darkest period in the island's history. In 1824, during the Greek war for independence, Turkish troops landed here unnoticed and caused a terrible blood bath, killing 1000 people. The survivors were enslaved.*

Once you have thoroughly enjoyed the beaches, wander 1.40 along to the chapel of Ay. **Konstantinos** ④. Utensils for the unforgettable evening consecration on the platform can be found in the annex. From here, stroll past the air- 2.15 port along the asphalt to reach the **fishing harbour in Fry** once again.

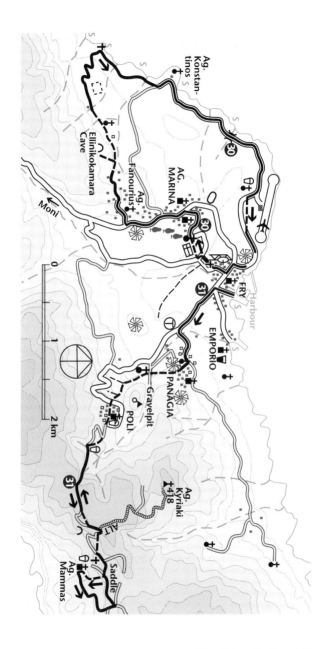

Ag. Konstan-tinos

Ellinikokamara Cave

Moni

Ag. Fanourius

AG. MARINA

30

30

FRY

Harbour

31

EMPORIO

PANAGIA

Gravelpit

POLI

Ag. Kyriaki
418

0

1

2 km

31

ALI

Ag. Mammas

Saddle

③ The Convent of Ayios Mámmas

An abandoned convent for nuns is situated high above the steep coast on the southern side of the island. It used to be reachable only along pack trails. A large white cross on the mountain ridge showed the pilgrim the way. In the meantime, there is also a dirt road here for visitors of the celebration of the church's consecration. The five-hour walk described here leads to this beautiful spot above the sea, avoiding the new way whenever possible. The ascent to 400 metres can be strenuous in hot weather. There is water at the church in Póli and in the convent itself. You must take along your own supplies of food.

▶ Map see previous page.

AWT	In **Fry**, you will be happy to turn your back on the over-
0.00	dimensional harbour and march uphill along the street to
0.10	the petrol station, where you turn left towards **Panagía**.

In the middle of the village, walk uphill behind the playground. On the right of the path, there is an unusual chapel lay-out – six next to one another ①. From the front, the little signs on the doors make it look like a group of attached houses – but the people living there are saints.

Leave the little street in a right curve further uphill and walk straight on to reach a monopáti, a bit overgrown, but leading nicely along the edge of the plains. It is inter-

0.25 rupted by a **street** leading to a gravel pit in the gorge, but its continuation on the other side is easy to find.

At the next fork, bear left upwards, accompanied by walls on both sides. At times the path goes along bare rock with steps hewn into it ②. At the fork beneath the village, take the path leading uphill to the left, cross the **street** and walk up to the right opposite the steep cement path and

0.35   into the maze of houses in **Póli**. This used to be the main village of the island, protected from pirates. After almost falling into ruins, the village has been able to recover. Next to the cemetery at the back end of the village, the

0.40   Church of the Holy Trinity, **Ayia Triáda**, awaits your visit. Its cistern offers a last chance to stock up on water before the ascent begins.

The wide dirt road leading up to the plateau begins on the right side of the church. Leave it again only three minutes later in the first sharp curve to the right to find a monopáti leading to the left and then uphill after a narrow spot. Later there is only a wall on the left, which you leave, going uphill to the right to wander up further along

0.55   a pack trail on the slope. Near some walls and an old **cistern**, you come to the dirt road again, which was laid over the old trail from this point on. It mounts without any major curves. Many old terraces in the fields extend down to the valley below. Above them on the left is the church at the peak, Ay. Kiriakí. You encircle the valley in a wide curve to the left, but leave the dirt road to the left (arrow) in the first sharp curve to the right. The old pack trail is there again – it leads upwards in a short-cut, and then you follow the dirt road to the left again.

1.10   *Alternative:* The following **turn-off** to the left leads, in a quarter of an hour, to the chapel at the peak, **Ayios Kiriakí**, a donation from a London ship magnate who originally came from Kássos. The chapel offers a magnificent view over to Kárpathos.

About 80 m after this turn-off, you can follow an arrow to the left and shorten the way along the dirt road again. This path is fairly stony, however, and ends up at the road again. Disregard a turn-off to the left, and soon you will

1.20 find yourself on the **ridge**, with a house on the right. At times a roaring wind rages here. After the ridge, your next way is along the second, more indistinct turn-off to the

1.25 right. This path leads to a little **pump house**, where you
★ have a view directly down to the convent situated gloriously above the sea ③.

*The **convent of Ayios Mámmas** is dedicated to the goatherds' saint, who, at the petition of the nuns, also transformed three Turkish pirate ships threatening the convent into the three rocks lying down in the sea.*

It was normally more peaceful here: the lovely garden with a good cistern and an eternal view of the sea from an altitude of 360 m seem to make the convent float in the heavens.

Nothing is known about the time of its origin. The wonderful, renovated pebble mosaics in the church's floor are particularly impressive. They show two lions and the double-headed eagle of the Byzantines.

For the way back, select the longer, more comfortable dirt road on the mountain. It offers tremendous views of the rocky coast and the Bay of Thýra. At the top, walk to the left at the fork. To the right, you could wander to the island's end at Aktí.

1.40 Soon you will be back on the **ridge** and begin the descent. At the walled-in olive grove, you come to the cistern

2.15 again (right) and the short-cut to **Póli** ④. This time it is

2.50 probably more relaxing to walk along the street to **Fry**!

Kastellórizo

This tiny island on the eastern edge of Europe is astonishingly cosmopolitan. This may come from the island's many different masters in the last century: the Turks, the French, the English and the Italians. And also certainly from the forced exodus of the population to Cyprus and Egypt during the last war. In the Golden Twenties, "Castellorizon" served as a landing place for French seaplanes from and to India and had a legendary reputation as Mikró Parísi, Little Paris.

As the wanderer enters the inviting harbour, his heart skips a beat when he sees the harsh vertical cliffs rising up behind the little city. You can wander comfortably on the plateau, however, although there is little shade and no usable cisterns there. The few shops offer everything you need for your tour - even a good map of the island for further exploration.

㉜ Edge of Europe

This easy walk along the coast takes two and a half hours and leads to a chapel at the edge of Europe. You return with a magnificent view of the harbour and the cliffs towering behind it. There are no springs.

AWT
0.00

At the **harbour**, leave the boats bobbing on the right and walk towards the north. A wide path upwards begins behind a gate after the post office and the big hotel. It leads

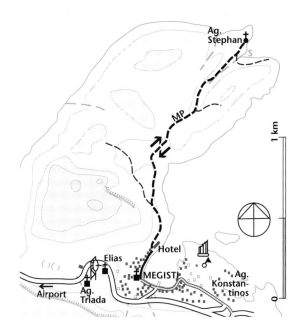

through an olive grove, with a lovely view of the islands located in front of it, and then continues above the coast. Bear right at a fork to reach, without any orientation problems, the little church of **Saint Stephan**. It is located on the peak of a cliff, like an outpost of Christianity facing the Asian continent. The Greek military forces use this spot, too, so that the Turks won't take them by surprise, but the inhabitants of Kastellórizos enjoy shopping in Kas, the Turkish village facing them.

0.50

If you walk back a few metres, you can get into the water from the flat rocks there.

Return along the same lovely path you came on, with a beautiful view of **Megisti.**

1.40

▶ **Hotel tip:** Pension Caretta (Tel: 224 60-492 08). A German-Greek/Australian couple offers tastefully furnished rooms in several buildings.

㉝ Patitíri – Ancient Winepresses

In ancient times, Megístí (its former name, which meant "the greatest") was at least great in viticulture. Cavities cut in the cliffs for pressing wine are still preserved. You will find some of them, visit a decaying fortified convent and climb up the Dorian acropolis. You need three to four hours and a lot of water to accomplish all this. The way is about five kilometres long, with a difference in altitude of 250 m. Before the walk, you can try to get the key to the convent of Saint George. With a few useful connections, this is sometimes possible in the pension "Krystallo" or in the taverna "Little Paris".

AWT
0.00

★

0.15

At the top of the village, on the right next to the church of Saint George (to the field), walk vigorously up the street and then go up a stone stairway opposite the street junction ①. A magnificent path of steps (picture on rear book cover) leads slowly upwards through the rocks. From here, you can look out far across the sea over to the Turkish city of Kas. The steps end at the **plateau**.

You can easily find the red-coloured path to the south here, up on the left of a fenced-in field. Walk to the left in front of the fortified convent ②. Directly next to the path, on the left in the rocks, there is a horizontal shaft with a fore chamber - an ancient grave now used as a goat pen.

0.25
*The fortified convent **Ayios Geórgios tou Bounioú** (Saint George on the Mountain), built in 1790, has been abandoned and is slowly decaying. Through a breach in the wall, you can see the courtyard with its windows shaped*

like loopholes for shooting and the church standing alone, the katholikón. If you have the key, you can see the icons of Saint George on the iconostasis in the church, next to Mary on the left at the end.

An exciting entry into a dark, narrow opening leads down to a grotto crypt dedicated to Saint Charálampos, "The Radiant". Salutory water drips from the walls.

60 to 70 m south of the convent, behind a fenced-in field, there is another sight worth seeing: a "patitíri", an ancient winepress ③.

At least three circular cavities were cut into large, almost flat rocks. One hollow had no drain, and two were connected by a groove. Archaeologists explain their function as follows: first the grapes were placed into the hollow without a drain, where they were pressed to a certain extent by their own weight. A very sweet wine was produced from this juice.

Then the grapes were pressed in wooden rings in the upper hollow by the stamping of feet, with the mash running into the lower hollow and collecting there. So far 47 such patitíri have been found on the island.

The way leads from the monastery to the quadratic drinking trough for animals located in the hollow and from there to the right, onto the shady field. Turn to the left here before a house, over a stone wall and onto an easily found path to the right. At the intersection with a diagonal path, turn left behind a water trough directly above

0.40 where the slope breakings off to reach the **Cyclopean Wall**.

Cyclopean Walls are enormous stones layered on one another without horizontal joints running through them and without mortar. This one comes from the Mycenean Era (1500 to 1300 BC) and elongated the natural cliff wall to extend to the rift.

Short Cut: From here you can go downhill to reach the cloister Ay. Triáda in eight minutes.

A mule track directly next to the wall leads slightly uphill to the right inland away from the gully to the (locked)

0.50 church of **Ay. Ioannis**.

Shortly before it, directly along the monastery's fence on the right of the path, you will discover another, even more nicely executed patitíri. (The second one in this area can hardly be found.)

The path goes uphill on the right of the solitary olive tree. In the beginning it is difficult to find, but it becomes broader later on and leads up to the **dir road**. Walking along it to the right, you come to the ridge, keenly watched by the soldiers on Mount Vígla. A foot path leads downhill exactly opposite the junction, on the right of the walled-in church of Saint Panteleimos and up to the **Paleókastro** ④.

0.55

1.05

> *This place has been fortified since very early times, nowadays even more, of course. The Dorians added gigantic square hewn stones to the massive walls of their city, which was dedicated to Apollo. In Byzantine times, quarry stone walls were consolidated over them. In our times, cement is used for the foundations of the gun positions. The three chapels form a peaceful compensation for the military surroundings.*
>
> *The many, sometimes immense, cisterns with a smooth finish on the inside are interesting. Thirst was certainly the most dangerous enemy of the citadel's inhabitants.*

Only the airport grounds impair the tremendous view: the mountains in Asia Minor and the many islets in front of them, the larger island of Ro in the west, where, completely alone, the country woman Déspina held the ground for Greece from 1927 to 1962. There is a monument to her at the beginning of this walking tour.

Return to the ridge under the Vígla and walk to the left from there, using steps down into the valley. After a few metres along the street, you come to the former monastery of **Ayía Triáda** (the Sacred Trinity, built in 1898). In the monastery's impressive courtyard paved with pebbles, you

1.25

can have the cloister church opened for you and admire the remarkable icons to the Trinity.

Afterwards, on the cliff in front of the neighbouring monastery of **Ayios Elias**, built in 1758, you can dream a little before walking along the flagstone path, the street and taking the short-cut through the houses to return to the wide **natural harbour**.

★

1.35

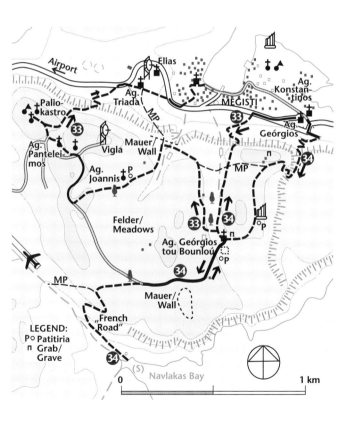

㉞ **The French Road**

This easy three-hour walking tour leads to a relic of World War I, past an archaic settlement and to the abandoned Monastery of Ayios Geórgios tou Bounioú. With a bit of luck, you will be able to get the keys to the monastery ㉝. The length of the stretch is about six kilometres, the difference in altitude 250 m. Don't forget drinking water!

▶ Map on previous page.

AWT
0.00 At the upper square in the city, walk uphill between the **church** to Saint George (to the field) and the monument to Déspina, the "country woman of Ro", in order to reach the street. At the street, go to the right and then immediately to the left onto a dirt road. From here, stone steps lead upwards into rocky terrain. From the lovely steps, you can see the city of Kas on the Turkish coast. After the

0.15 **last steps**, walk straight on with a stone wall on your left. You wander along a flat stretch for a short while to reach a winding path to the right which leads to an even higher flat area.

At the top, you see a round construction on the right of the slope. This is an ancient grave which was used as a shelter by the Italians in the war and serves as a goat pen nowadays.

From there, wander to the south along the plateau, and soon you will notice large, round Cyclopean Walls (left). The round constructions date back to the 6th century BC and are part of an archaic settlement. 50 m afterwards, on

the left of the path, there is a patitíri, an ancient wine-press, as described in ㉝. The path leads on to the right at

0.35 the fork, to the **Monastery of Ayios Geórgios tou Bounioú**. See ㉝.

After finding a patitíri there, too, walk to the southwest along the dirt road until you come to a solitary olive tree and then continue to the left along the "French Road" down into the valley.

The French built these well-preserved ramps ① in World War I in order to haul heavy artillery up to the plateau. Turkey, at that time allied with Germany, represented a threat to France, which needed the island as a stepping stone for its Indian possessions.

0.55 The ramp ends at the **rocky bay of Navlákas** ②, an an-choring area in World War I. You can get to the deep water directly from the cliff there, with a bit of difficulty, but should not swim out too far and should not be alone due to climbing out again.

1.15 Return the same way, but with the **Monastery** of Saint George on the right, and wander straight along a clearly visible path above a hollow full of trees until you reach the edge of the cliff. There you will find another set of

1.45 steps down into the village of **Megísti**.

Níssiros

Island connoisseurs are ecstatic when they hear this name. The volcanic island has hardly any beaches worth mentioning and is thus more natural and original than the surrounding islands. Day-excursionists from Kos arrive at 11 am and depart again at 4 pm. Then the island belongs to the locals and their guests once again. There aren't many of these, so you soon meet people, at the latest in the evening at the romantic main square in Mandráki, the Platía Ilikioméni.

The interior of the island is "hollow". A gigantic caldera, a crater, is located inside. It came into being long ago when an immense cavern caved in. The island's rim is formed by a ring of mountains and is very fertile. Wandering along it is delightful. When the weather is not clear, you must be careful in the mountains because of the fog and clouds.

In the hotels, there is a small leaflet "Information-Map" free of cost with information and a good map of the island.

㉟ On the Volcano

You climb over the edge of the crater along old paths and wander down onto the volcano's flat plains before you descend even further, to where the earth's crust is only a few centimetres thick and the smell of sulphur tickles your nose. Later, you return along the island's rim.

The strenuous five-to-six-hour walk covers 13 km and can be shortened in the middle, but check the bus schedule first!

AWT   If you want to shorten the tour by an hour, you can take a taxi to the **Monastery of Evangelistra**. Otherwise, follow the description in ㊱ to reach it.

0.50   A narrow, fenced-in lane leads away from the gigantic **terebinth tree** in front of the monastery ①. At its end, walk to the right, still along the fence, and then downhill along a path from which a deep valley-floor, Káto Lákki, can be seen on the left. Cross over the dirt road you come to and wander uphill along the Profitis Elias massif. Then

1.15   walk downhill again to reach a **ridge**, with the green plains of the caldera ② soon beneath you, dominated by the monastery of Ioánnis Theológos on the other side of the crater. A wide, irregularly marked gravel path leads

1.35   down through olive terraces to the **street**, which you follow to the right. Experimental geothermic drilling grounds are located above on the right. Economic utilisation of the earth's heat has failed so far due to the popula-

1.45   tion's rejection. Then you come to the **kiosk** under shady trees.

Till now, you have taken no notice of the main attraction: where lines of tourists disappear and reappear, there is a gigantic, almost circular hole, Stefan's Crater. As you go down into it, the odour of sulphur from within the ground becomes more intensive. Once you are down below, you notice that, at some spots, the caldera's ground is only about 20 cm thick. Muddy grey water bubbles underneath. This is the largest of a total of five craters which can be visited. The last time the volcano was active was in 1888. As on Milos und Santorini, the European and African continental plates meet here, which keeps leading to earthquakes. The most recent was in 1933.

Short-Cut: Return from the kiosk by bus.

Alternative: If you are looking for a nice spot to rest above the caldera ③, walk up towards the south-east at first, without a path, to the dirt road leading to the **Monastery of Stavros**. From there, walk downhill for 5 minutes, until you reach the path described below at AWT 2.15.

The direct way to Mandráki continues on along the dusty, white dirt road in the same direction, crosses through a farmyard and leads into an elevated foot path behind it, which goes up into a dry gully and then meanders through the rocks. You need the practised eye of an island wanderer here to recognise the partially overgrown path.

2.15   After a portal, take the **dirt road** to the right, passing a chapel (right). This sandy road, unfortunately in an excessive width at times, leads along above the sea, then across a broad green ridge with the ruins of a hamlet and to the north along the island's outer rim. You can see far out across the sea and recognise Astipálea and other small islets. Behind the helicopter landing area, continue straight

3.45   on at the fork to get to **Paleókastro**, the ancient "castle".

It is still disputed whether the walls protected a city or only an acropolis. In any case, the gigantic stone blocks which were fitted together exactly here and the well preserved gate are impressive.

Opposite the entry path to the castle gate, a narrow foot

3.55   path leads down to **Mandráki**.

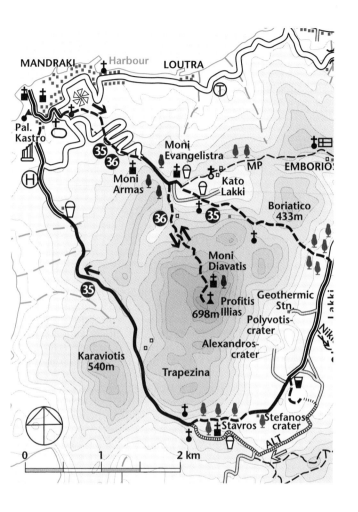

㊱ The Monastery on the Peak

For this four-to-five-hour ascent to the peak, you need no Alpine climbing ability but a certain amount of energy. An abandoned monastery with a view across the islands is located at the top. Picnic lovers should take along drinks and food, of course.

▶ Map on previous page.

AWT
0.00
0.08

0.30

0.40
0.50

Heading away from the sea, walk uphill in a gentle curve to the left along the street directly under the **monastery in Mandráki** until you come to a **fork in the road**. Continue uphill to the right past the wayside shrine (right) for 60 m. *Before* a chapel, turn left onto a very narrow path ① (arrow). A sufficient number of red dots and arrows allow you to appreciate the lovely agricultural terraces with their stonework. Oaks and fig cacti offer shade along the wonderful, gently mounting path. Cross the **street** and look for the connecting path on the other side right away. You meet it two more times before walking along the **street** to arrive at the **Evangelistria Monastery**, the cloister of the Annunciation of the Virgin Mary.

If the cloister church is open, you can admire its lovely fittings and a very valuable icon. There is a fountain in the forecourt.

A gigantic tree, a terebinth, stands in front of the cloister. ㊱ turns off here.

Walk back 60 m. A footpath marked with red dots turns off the street to the left here, leading uphill to the south – don't confuse it with the dirt road on the left of it! It leads

leisurely uphill, past ruins (left), and is easily recognisable with stone cairns as markers. Below on the right there is a small, deep valley-floor. The path ② mounts slowly and
1.20 later becomes a true delight under shady **kermes oaks**.
1.40 Ferns line the path up to the wildly romantic **Diavátis Monastery** located in a hollow ③ high above the sea. The author has constructed a bench for his readers in front of the monastery.

There are only footpaths between kermes oak bushes up
1.50 to the chapel of **Profítis Elías** ④ at the peak. From the surveyed point (698 m), you can see Kos in the north and, behind it, Kálymnos and Psérimos. In the east there is the Turkish peninsula Resadiye, on which the ancient Greek city of Kidnos was located. Tílos is in the south, and, in the west behind three smaller islands, you can see lovely Astipálea. There is still a lot of wandering awaiting there!
3.20 You need 1.5 hours back to **Mandráki**.

㊲ Greek Sauna

From Páli, you walk up to the rim of the crater in a pleasant four-hour tour, wander along the outer-most wall of the ring and return to Mandráki. In addition, you can discover a natural sauna and a wonderful restaurant on the rim of the volcano!

AWT 0.00 The bus quickly takes you to the tranquil fishing harbour of **Páli**. Walk inland along the **eastern mole**, turn to the left with the street and immediately to the right again ①. The little street mounts slightly and is soon covered in white. If you walk to the left at the steps, you arrive at a building where the white splendour suddenly ends and a 0.05 somewhat dilapidated **set of steps** begins. Later leading 0.12 along rubble, it takes you up to the **street**.

Alternative: The way described from this point on requires a certain amount of pioneer spirit as well as long trousers. If you would rather take a more comfortable way, continue along the street to the left from here on to arrive at a water reservoir ④ (= AWT 0.35). in less than 25 minutes. Immediately after it, continue uphill to the right along the paved path.

The old monopáti continues on the other side of the street, but two metres higher ②. It is, however, rather overgrown after a few metres, so, for safety's sake, you should use the fence on the left as a guide. When the fence turns off to the left, continue uphill on a mule track 0.20 and then bear left at the fork. At a red **arrow** on the left wall, leave the monopáti to the left. A chapel ③ visible somewhat higher on the left is the next destination. The

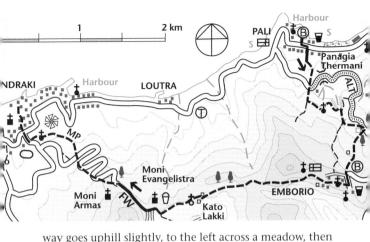

way goes uphill slightly, to the left across a meadow, then 50 m later through a gully made of pumice-stone and along narrow paths to the **chapel**. The footpath continues beneath it and then circles around a green hollow and a rugged ravine, also out of pumice-stone. There are caves beneath the path, so be careful! Across the ridge of a slope, you come to a footpath running parallel to the street and to a large **reservoir** ④ directly next to the street.

On the other side, a delightful old paved path winds its way uphill under oak trees to **Emborio**. 80 m later, on the right of the street, there is a natural sauna.

The room made of layered stones is 1.50x1.50 m in size and is hellishly hot. The steam comes from the volcano's heat and is released between the moss-covered stones.

0.25

0.35

★
0.50

The taverna "Baltani" located next to the church offers refreshingly cool drinks and delicious food as well as a fantastic view into the volcano's crater.

Steps lead up to the ghost town, which was abandoned after the earthquake in 1933 when most of its inhabitants moved down to Páli. In the past few years, however, life has returned to some of the ruins.

1.00 The path leads through the last pale blue ruins, below the **upper church** and on out of the village, with the valley on your left. It continues straight on at the steps on the right leading up to the cemetery. Parts of the original path have slid down, but there are numerous red markings indicating detours. Beneath the peak, wander past an inter-

1.15 esting grey rock formation until you **notice the sea** down on the right. Now walk downhill, with a view of the har-

★ bour of Mandráki, and arrive at a plateau with olive trees and oaks under which you can have a splendid rest ⑤. Your eye roves from the pumice-stone island of Gyáli to the long island of Kos and even further to Kálymnos and Psérimos.

1.35 The path continues above the deep valley of Káto Lakki (left), crosses through a dilapidated **farmyard** and then a narrow pass between two fences and finally arrives at the

1.45 **Evangelistra Monastery** ⑥, which is usually locked shut (see ㊱).

At the gigantic terebinth tree, walk along the dirt road until you come to the first right curve, where you will find a marked turn-off to the left along a footpath. It meets the street twice, crosses it once and finally ends up in

2.30 **Mandráki**.

Psérimos

A tranquil island – after 5 pm when the day-excursionists from Kos have left. From the island of Kálymnos, you can reach Psérimos by a small daily ship. From Kos arrange a passage on an excursion craft instead of taking the "Three Island Tour". There is a surplus of tavernas and a sufficient number of beds in the low season.

㉛ A Deserted Beach

This leisurely two-hour walking tour can be done with ease during a day-excursion. You wander to the interior of the island along a dirt road and later, walking on goat paths, arrive at the long sandy beach and the chapel of Panagía Grafiótissa. There are no cisterns along the way.

AWT
0.00   The dirt road to the interior of the island begins directly at the **harbour** and leads past the tavernas and the church of the Assumption of the Virgin (Panagía), where architectural fragments of the early Christian church can be
0.10   seen in the forecourt. At the **fork** in front of a group of pines, bear left, and then left again at the next fork at the end of the grove.

Now you can "enjoy" the Greek countryside: walking through a little valley with unimaginative houses and carefully scattered remains of used items, heading for a farm. From there, the dirt road goes uphill to the left until
0.20   you arrive at the **ruins of a farmstead** (left).

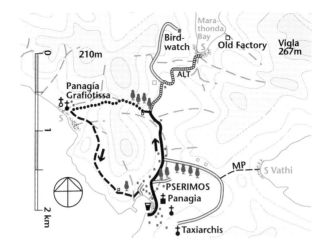

Alternative: If you stay on the dirt road and walk
downhill to the right further up it, you walk through a
lovely valley-floor and arrive after 20 minutes at **the
pebble-sand beach of Marathónda**, lined with
greenery and with the remains of a tile factory.

The new house visible up on the hill in front on the left
is used for the observation of migratory bird swarms.
The wander route crosses through the **ruins** of the farmstead, leads through the group of trees on the left and then
along comfortable goat paths up to the bedraggled tree on
0.35   the **ridge**. The terrain rim remains about 80 m below on
the left. From here, you have a view of the islands of Platís
and Kálymnos and of a chapel on the beach (photo left).
Along a goat path on the left above the ditch, you arrive
0.55   safe and sound at the **Chapel of Panagía Grafiótissa**. At
the second chapel, you can see what happens if you don't
build on St. Peter's rock. Down below, you see the expanse
of a long sandy beach, deserted because the excursion
boats can't land in the shallow water. And who would
think of walking all this way? Now you can stretch out
and relax.

Walk back along the seaside, at first on the left of a hill
near the coast. Shortly before the harbour, you can see the
ruins of a farm and then walk down to the sandy beach of
1.25   **Psérimos-Chóra**. The inn-keepers are waiting.

Sími

The once prosperous city is beginning to blossom again. After it had been abandoned to ruin for a long time, tourism has given it back its distinguished character. Many houses have been renovated (photo page 19). Primarily British and Scandinavian holiday makers feel extremely contented here. The prices are respectable.

Outside of the colourful harbour village, the landscape offers more lovely sights: large monasteries, shady pine forests and many old mule tracks. While wandering, you should take into account that Sími is hotter than the other islands and, at the same time, rather hilly. For longer stays, you can purchase two wander brochures.

㊲ The Chapel of Ayios Vassílios

High above the blue sea, a tiny church is hidden in the cliff. You will discover it and, in addition, a broad, deserted bay for swimming. You will need a total of five to six hours, a lot of water and perhaps some food. You walk along monopátia and well-marked footpaths. Due to its length and the ascent, the walking tour is strenuous in the heat.

Excursion boats sometimes go to the Bay of Vassilios, and you may possibly be able to pre-arrange the return.

AWT At the southern edge of the **harbour of Gialós**, take the
0.00 second lane leading inland, pass by the church's cam-

panile (left) and turn left opposite the sport field. From there, find your way on the right of the castle mountain towards the antennas on the mountain peak and look for the wide, steep set of stairs that is still in the shadow of the castle mountain in the morning. The stairs are called Kataráktis – waterfalls – which says everything. At the top, turn right and head for the upper of the two churches. In front of this church, you will find dots marking the way and then continue up more steps to the right or simply ask someone about the "monopáti".

You soon leave the houses behind and can enjoy a fantastic view of the lovely city. Bear right at the fork after the
0.30   gate! The delightful, rocky path ① leads to the **Chapel of Ayía Paraskeví**, the protector of eyes. Your first break on the shady dancing area comes just at the right time.

The monopáti has been renovated to more than perfect condition from this point on and leads to the street through a sparse little forest of kermes oaks. The
0.40   **Monastery of Michail Perivilótis** across the way is shut and forces you to turn off to the left.

At the corner of the entrance to the monastery gardens, turn right onto a cement path which leads through fields blessed with numerous chapels. This is the zenith, at 275 m above sea-level. The cement ends at the
0.50   **Monastery of Ayios Nikoláos** which is hidden among trees. From here, a dirt road leads downhill to a **gate**. Before it, walk to the left, following the colourful dots. They
★   lead you safely downhill towards the sea on the right side of the ravine. Above the sea, you walk through a wildly romantic landscape with sparse woods ② and can see the
1.15   beach. After the shady woods, there are **ruins** on the left

of the path, which then makes a left curve towards the sea. Wandering above the shining blue sea, you shouldn't
1.25 miss the **Chapel of Ayios Vassílios**, St. Blasius ③, below on the right of the path! Steps lead down to a wonderful spot to sit above the sea. The church has old frescoes, which are unfortunately very sooty. All the utensils needed for a proper consecration of the church are stored in the little building across from it.

The rest of the way to the beach ④ is without a path and steep, but without arousing feelings of vertigo. Down be-
1.35 low at the long **bay**, there are pebbles and sand and, normally, except for caïque boats, not a soul. Enjoy it - you have really earned this.

1.55 Return the same way, past the **ruins**, next to the ravine to
2.25 the **dirt road** and through the fields in front of the **Peri-**
2.35 **vilótis Monastery**.

You can go down to the right to the city here – this is the way with the better view! (35 minutes)

If you still want to take a little detour, walk to the left
2.45 along the flat street and turn right at the **cement street** to arrive at the locked Fanoúrios Monastery, where another
3.20 old mule track leads down to **Gialós**.

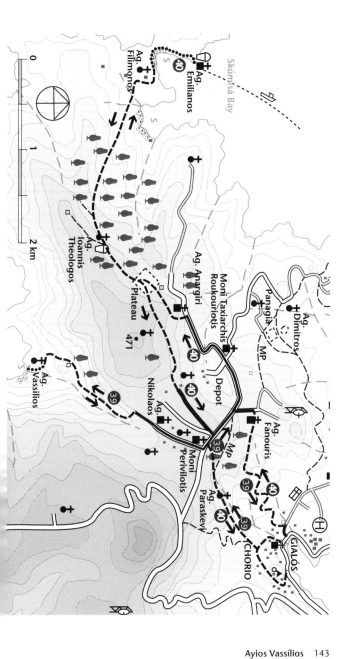

⑳ The Monastery in the Sea

For the loveliest walking tour on the island, you need six to seven hours and perseverance – Sími can be hot! A mighty fortified monastery and a monastery on an island can be seen. Longer stretches lead through a low pine forest without great ascents.

As a short-cut, you can try to organise your return on the daily excursion boat or have yourself fetched by a caïque for the return trip from Ay. Emilianós.

▶ Map on previous page.

AWT At the bridge in the harbour, the street leads inland on the
0.00 left of the square. The abandoned barrel-vaulted building with a double nave on the left before the next square is the former ice factory. Before the street mounts, even before the grey water tank, walk up a lane on the left to reach an old mule track further uphill. It winds its way up
0.35 to the small, locked **Monastery of Ayios Fanoúris**.
Then take the cement path to the left to reach the street and walk to the right along this street in a wide left curve
0.50 to arrive at the **Monastery of Taxiárchis Michaélis Roukouriótis** ①.

A sacred shrine was located here in antique times. The present fortified monastery from the 15th century presents exterior walls which are almost completely closed and, on the interior, a series of terraces set around the two-storey katholikón. The upper church has frescoes of all the saints, and, one by one, they have been "smoked" by the

*country woman living in the monastery. Especially the
icons and carvings from the 18th century are remarkable.
The main attraction is the archangel Michael in em-
bossed silver on the right of the iconostasis. He is fighting
evilness with the sword; in his left hand, he holds a child
symbolising the soul. He is the island's patron saint.*

*If the country woman wants to find the key, for the lower
church, you can view frescoes there, too, but in bad condition.*

When you leave the monastery, walk around the big tree
and down the cement street. After the military depot
(left), you quickly come to the charming but locked

1.00   **Monastery of Ayía Anárgiri**.

Above the monastery walls, red dots draw your attention
1.15   to an old stone path which leads slowly uphill to a **square**
!!   surrounded by stones. Don't walk straight through the
square! The clever wanderer turns about 45° to the left
and looks for red markings on the stone wall pointing to
right and then meanders through a pine forest ② to the

1.30   **Chapel of Áyios Ioánnis Theólogos** ③. You have already
seen today's destination down in the water, the
monastery in the sea. But first there is a short break in
front of the chapel!

Directly below it, you head downhill. Three minutes later,
!!   be sure not to miss the path downhill to the right. Now
you are approaching your goal ④.

Down at the bottom, walk without a path and, before the
2.10   fence on the right, uphill to the **Monastery of Áyios Filí-
monos**. Ask the friendly fisherman who lives here
whether you can look at the old frescoes in the little
barrel-vaulted church.

Cement steps lead to the sandy bay. Stepping on one of the numerous sea-urchins wouldn't, of course, be very advantageous for wandering on.

2.25   *The **Monastery of Áyios Emilianós** is located on an adjacent rocky island. In the pleasant courtyard, you can imagine spending a few days in a monastery. At the stone table on the island's end, you could polish your plans for the future.*

But there's not much time for sitting around today. Take
3.25   the same way back, walking above the **chapel to St. John**
3.40   until you return to the **square**.

Alternative: The rest of the way described below leads through rocks and is somewhat difficult. You can take the same, more comfortable return route along the street, missing, however, the lovely view over to the Turkish mainland.

In the **square**, there are markings indicating the way uphill to the right. If you don't miss any of the red dots in the
4.05   pointed rocks, you arrive at a **farmstead** with a chapel on the ridge and then take the dirt road downhill on the oth-
4.15   er side of the mountain to the closed **Perivilótis Monastery**.

On the other side of the street, another monopáti, 20 m off to the right, leads down into the valley. After passing the double chapel of **St. Paraskeví** and requesting good eyesight from her, you can see the beautiful town of Sími.
4.35   You soon come to the upper section, **Chorió**.

According to the amount of energy you still have left, you can take the steep staircase (kataráktis) on the left *before* the kástro down to Gialós or the longer but nicer Kalí Stráta ("Good Street") to the harbour. Phew!

Short walking tour for a day-excursion:
Follow the description above uphill to the **Fanoúris Monastery** (AWT 0.35), walk to the left along the cement path until you come to the **main street** and then go up to the left to the **Monastery of Perivilotis** (right.). Turn to the left there along a monopáti leading to the church of Ay. Paraskeví (AWT 4.10) and then back to the harbour with a beautiful view. Total time: 1.5 to 2 hours.

▶ "Sími Tours" (near the harbour) offer several combination tours with wandering and boats. Tel 224 60-713 07.

㊶ Around Emborió

*Five hours are necessary to discover the hilly area
north of Sími. The paths are easy to find, the ascents
are slight and there is a place where you can stop for
refreshments, so the tour is not difficult. But there
are no fountains.*
*The tour can be shortened by taking the taxi boat
from Emborió.*

AWT 0.00   At the **bridge in Giálos**, walk inland along the left of the
square, turn slightly to the right, pass the old barrel-vaulted ice factory and then breathe heavily as you go up the
street ① to the right. The grey water tank is on the left. Af-

0.10   ter the cemetery (left), turn onto a **footpath to the left**. It
is marked in blue and red and mounts in a curve to the

0.15   right. After a **gate**, you pass a house (right) and look down
upon the bay of Emborió ②. Walk above the broad valley
in a wide arc halfway up the mountain. Before a long field
wall, there is a sort of fork in the path – go up to the left
here and then over the hill.

!!   Pay attention about 50 m after the hill – be sure not to
overlook the *turn-off down to the right*. It leads between two
gardens with walls and then to the right through a dry

0.50   stream bed and uphill to the chapel of **Ayios Dimítrios**.
Directly after the chapel, leave the street downhill towards the right and turn to the left shortly afterwards in
order to arrive at the next summit, where you are at the
dirt road again. Wander along it to the right. The way

0.55   forks after a bunker (left), but, *shortly before it*, a **footpath
turns off to the left**.

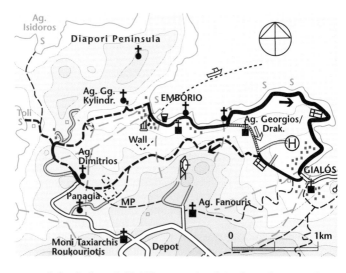

It leads downhill 130 metres in altitude to the sea, where
1.10 you arrive at a stone house at the **beach of Tolí**. The
boats don't come here; you are usually alone. The pebbles
are smaller on the southern part of the beach on the left.
1.30 When you are **up above again**, walk along the dirt road
towards Emborió and, after a few metres, take the footpath on the right down into the valley. There are field
walls and fences on the right of the path. After passing
through a gate, meander to the left almost horizontally
above a sharp incision in the terrain and then uphill to
1.50 the closed chapel of **Ayios Geórgios Kylindriotis** for the
view.
From there, climb through the boulders to the sea near
2.00 **Emborió** and to the right along the beach.

*If you follow the dry stream bed inland after 70 m, you
arrive at the only worthwhile sight. 50 m away from the
sea, turn off to the left to climb lovely steps to a triple
chapel. Roman-early Christian **mosaics** have been found
on the right of it.*

*If you continue in this direction, coloured markings lead
to twelve subterranean vaults. A **school for painting
icons** is said to have existed here. If the filled-up openings
for windows were exposed, this could be imagined. Otherwise, they would probably have been pretty dark saints.*

2.05   Further along the beach, the nice **taverna** "Metapontis" offers a rather cramped seaside life.

   Short-cut: A taxi-boat leaves from here for Giálos at 4pm and 5pm.

From the taverna, walk further on the cement way along the sea. Nímos, the neighbouring island on the left, can hardly be distinguished from Sími. Two monasteries on the beach can be seen – but each is on a different island.

2.15   *Short-cut:* After a newly constructed **wall** made of quarry stone (right), marked cement steps turn off up-hill on the right. Walk past the **Monastery of Ayios Geórgios Drakoundiótis** and through the fields along paths lined with walls to reach **Gialós** in about 25 minutes.

The cement way along the seaside is nicer. With the sea on your left, meander along, with a few bathing areas to choose from, and enjoy the grand finale. With the sun astern, navigate into the harbour and anchor at one of the

2.55   restaurants after the **bridge in Gialós**.

Tílos

The traveller is greeted by the wide bay around the harbour city of Livádia. The gently modelled island shows hardly any rough cliffs here, only several green areas. A pleasant, tranquil kind of tourism is enjoyed here. Not only most of the individual tourists come from England but also a colourful, precise map of the island, which can be purchased in the stores. The numerous springs are very useful during the walking tours. Some mule tracks have been restored, while others have disappeared under the bulldozers' shovels.

④ Mikro Chório

Mikro Chório means "small village". It is, however, rather a small city which hasn't been inhabited since 1967 and is meanwhile in ruins. It is the destination of this easy five-hour walking tour, which then leads through a romantic ravine to the sea and returns, high above the coast, to Livádia.

AWT
0.00

In **Livádia**, the old path of steps on the right of the **taverna "Omonóia"** ("Harmony") leads up to Mikro Chório. Still in Livádia, it soon becomes a footpath before it meets up with a sandy road on top. Follow the sandy road to the

0.07

left. 50 m *before* the asphalt street, there is a **gate** you should pass through in order to wander further along the old path. Open and then shut the second gate before you arrive at the beautiful old monopáti ① leading further

0.17   uphill. It crosses the **street** and, somewhat later, a newer
0.20   **cement path**. Immediately after it, follow the wall but
      then turn off to the left to pass by the old spring house.
      The walls along the way are in ruins and slowly set you in
      the mood for a ghost town. You come to a dirt road and
0.40   walk up a few steps to a closed – **disco** – in the middle of
      the ruins. It is open nightly in July and August.

      The largest of the churches in the abandoned village has
      been renovated. The smaller one under the castle has very
      old frescoes. You look at the saints eye to eye – if divine

intervention allows you entrance. Walking through the narrow lanes, up and down the steps, is quite an experience in itself – especially in the evening atmosphere. After exploring, walk down the lane in front of the church, past two chapels (left) and, after 50 m, left towards the sea at a fork in the way. After the last ruins, before a rocky hill, walk straight on at a big kermes oak, leaving the rocks on your left. Walking in or next to a dry

0.55 stream bed, you arrive at the **street**.

Go through a gate on the other side of the street and walk downhill along a new dirt road – or, as a purist, in the dry bed set in a wall next to it on the right. Continue uphill to

1.05 the right at a lovely Greek **fountain** ②. At the *cairns 60 m*

!! *later,* plunge down to the left into a wildly romantic ra-

★ vine. Hopping between oleanders and boulders, you

1.30 arrive directly at **Léthra Bay** ③. If the pebbles are too big for you and the (few) other swimmers are too many, you can pick out another place to swim further on.

You arrive back at the ravine in five minutes and walk

1.35 **uphill to the left** along a path marked by thick cairns. When you see the Bay of Livádia again, thinner cairns point out that you go downhill there for eight minutes to reach **Amokhosti Bay** ④. You are usually alone here.

2.20 At the end, you return to **Livádia** along beautiful paths high above inaccessible bays.

In the taverna "Omonóia", quickly ask Maria what she is cooking this evening.

㊸ Neró

Water, "neró" in Greek, is only available in cisterns on many islands. During this walking tour, however, you pass by three springs whose cool water you can drink.
The strenuous tour takes five to six hours but can be shortened.

AWT
0.00

From the Italian **harbour building** in **Livádia**, meander along the Paralía and past the eating places. When you have circled the bay, turn right onto a dirt road leading uphill before you pass the taverna "Fáros" at the fishing

0.30
0.40

harbour of **Ayios Stéfanos**. At the top, you are greeted by the **Chapel of St. John** ☐ and a renovated kalderími ☐ will lead you on The wanderers' prayers have thus been heard by the tourist office. As you walk uphill, don't for-

★
0.55
!!
1.10

get to look back! (p. 150) Walk on the right of a ditch with oleander till a **fork**. If you go left here, you pass a dilapi-dated farmstead after the oleander ditch and must later be careful not to miss the **turn-off** ☐ to the left.

Alternative: If you continue straight on for 10 minutes, you come to the impressive village in ruins called **Ierá**, where only goats and ghosts still reside. The last families moved away around 1960.

1.25

Red markings help along the way down to the water, so you soon reach the **fountain**. It is said that water was found here by a priestly dignitary who was almost dying of thirst after a sea voyage. That's why this region is called Despóti Neró. There are two beaches here. The hot black pebbles would certainly cause Indian fire-walkers hellish

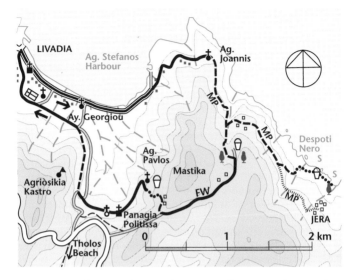

joy. Other people must first use cool sea water from a plastic bag in order to be able to sit there and enjoy the view of Kos.

2.00 Return the same way to the **oleander ditch**.

    Short-cut: From there, you can return to **Livádia** in a little more than an hour.

Walk uphill along the ditch to arrive at a walled-in grove guarded by cairns and go around it to the right. There is another fenced-in spring a few metres below. Behind the

2.10 grove, you meet up with a new **dirt road**, which you follow uphill on the left of the remains of the old footpath.

2.15 On the **ridge** (with the ruins of a house), you have a view over a gentle, hilly landscape and a peninsula – with the new rubbish depot. It is praiseworthy that rubbish should no longer be burned, but the architects of the Greek classical period would have constructed a temple here instead.

2.25 Continue along the dirt road, under which the earlier stone path is located, until you arrive at the next **ridge**. From here, you can see the Bay of Livádia again and, on the right at the same level, a few dilapidated houses which can be reached quickly along a goat path. At the trees in the second group of houses, a red marking indicates the beginning of the descent across the grazing ter-

2.40 races. Soon a large pine and the **Chapel of Ay. Pávlos** can be seen down below ④.

> *The chapel dominates the valley. Inside, however, you won't find any more icons. Instead, there is the polite request in perfect English to water the flowers with the chapel's spring water. It's nice to be of help.*

The way back leads to the closed **Monastery of Panagía Polítissa**. On only one day in the year, on Panigiri, 22 August, is, so to speak, hell let loose. From here, continue on to the fork, where you bear uphill to the left, turn to the

!! right in the curve and walk downhill along the old mule track, of course – after all, you are a wanderer.

3.20 **Livádia** is reached without any problems.

The way to lovely Thólos Beach:
From Livádia, first take the way described directly above. Walk uphill west of Panagía Polítissa, across the road on the ridge and downhill along the rocky path. See the map.

⑭ Áyios Panteleímonas

On this four to five-hour walking tour the only possible way on foot is a goat path through the phrýgana and then a stretch along the street to the beautiful monastery with a spring under shady trees.

AWT From **Ayios António s**, walk westwards along the street to
0.20 the **Kamariáni Monastery**, located in a lovely garden. 40 m after the garden walls, a footpath marked in red leads uphill to the left. The footpath passes through terraces,
0.40 leads past a **cistern** and then to lovely picnic spots under
!! olive trees. Afterwards, you have to pay careful attention:
0.50 **red arrows** point uphill to the left. After the ascent, continue a bit more pleasantly, walking slightly uphill to the
1.15 right until you reach the saddle with the **ruins of a chapel** whose most valuable part is the lintel. The way down
✓ leads along the island's harsh exterior, at times on the old steps. Sufferers of vertigo should perhaps busy themselves more with the vegetation on the left side rather than looking down at the sea. After a field of rubble, the path
1.40 continues safely to the street and on to the hidden **Mon-**
OW **astery of St. Panteleímonas** with a shady café.

> *The picturesque fortified monastery from the 14th century was inhabited until 1930. It then served as lodging for livestock keepers and was in danger of falling into ruin. Now freshly renovated, it presents itself as a castle keep, cell tract with arcades (left) and Byzantine katholikón. The carvings on the iconostasis are especially fascinating.*

It more relaxing to return on the street along the sea. Especially if you haven't forgotten your swimming gear.

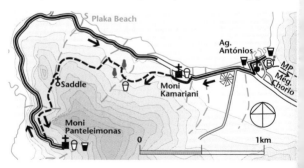

Island Hopping

The nicest way to discover the Greek islands is certainly by
approaching them from the sea. With the many connections
by ship, it is easy to drift from island to island. Boarding and
going ashore with almost all of the island's inhabitants taking
part is a special experience. Strong winds however, can whirl
the ferry schedules into disorder, so chance easily joins you as
a travelling companion on this kind of trip.

The **big ferries** are the most pleasant, with their large upper
deck which is usually used by tourists. The locals can usually
be seen in the salons and restaurants on the lower deck. The
reasonable prices are strongly subsidized.

In addition, there are smaller ships for lateral connections and
the fast **airfoil boats** and **catamarans**. Unfortunately, you
cannot sit outside on the latter and see very little of the sea
through the salt-encrusted windows. You pay about double
the price for this.

The **main route** for the big ferries, often with several daily
trips, goes between Rhodes, (not always to **Sími**), **Tílos,
Níssiros, Kos** to Kálymnos, and then leads to Piräus via the
Cycladian island of Amorgós.

Kárpathos along with **Kássos** and **Chálki** can only be reached
from Rhodes or Crete. This line goes to Piräus via Mílos.

Chálki also has a ferry connection to the harbour of Kámiros-
Skála on Rhodes, across from it.

Kastellórizo is linked with Rhodes by ship connection.

The daily excursion boats from **Kos** to **Níssiros** also leave from
the harbours of Kamári and Kardámena on Kos.

Small daily ships leave the harbour of Mastichári near the
airport on **Kos** for **Kálymnos**.

Psérimos can be reached most easily on the excursion boats
from Kos and Kálymnos.

There are several excursion boats daily from Rhodes to **Sími**.

Some Greek words for hikers:

Stress on the accents.

jássas	hello	kerós	**weather**
ne	yes	aéras	wind
óchi	no	meltémi	strong north wind
parakaló	please	ílios	sun
efcharistó	thank you	wrochí	rain
endáxi	okay	omíchli	fog
sto kaló	all the best		
kalá	lovely	níssos	**island**
símera	today	farángi, langádi	ravine, gorge
ávrio	tomorrow	kámpos, pláka	plains
pósin óra?	How long?	livádi	meadow
pósso makriá ine ja?	How far is it to...?	déndro	tree
		léfkes	poplars
puíne...?	Where is...?	dássos	forest
óra	hour	lófos	hill
neró	water	wounó, óros	mountain
psomí	bread	vígla	mountain peak
tirí	cheese	vráches	rock, cliff
míkro	small	spíleo	cave
mégalo	big	thálassa	sea
leoforió	bus	órmos	bay
stásis	bus stop	límni	lake
enikáso	rent	potámi	river
aftókinito	auto	réma	dry bed
mechanáki	motor bike	pigí	spring
podílato	bicycle	pérazma	pass, ridge
kaíki	boat	xirolithía	dry wall
chóra	**city**	odiporió	**wandering**
chorió	hamlet	isía	straight on
spíti	house	dexiá	right
platía	square	aristerá	left
parélia	harbour promenade	apáno	uphill
kástro	Venetian castle	káto	downhill
pírgos	fortified Venetian castle	kondá	near
		makriá	far
nekrotafío	cemetery	ásfalto	asphalt street
limáni	harbour	drómos	street
vrísi	fountain	chomaódromos	gravel street
stérna	cistern	dasikí odós	forest path
kafenío	café, and how!	odós	path
		skála	path of steps
eklisiá	**church**	monopáti	mule track
papás	priest	kalderími	paved way
moní, monastíri	monastery	katsikó drómos	goat path
ksoklísi	chapel	yéfira	bridge
panagía	Mother of God	stavrodrómi	crossing, intersection
panigíri	parish fair		
ágios, agía, AG	saint	hártis	map
ikonostasio	icon altar screen	kutrúmbulo	path marking
katholikón	central building in a monastery	phrýgana	scrub, the island hiker's enemy

Abbreviations, Key

━━━━━	hiking route on a road or dirt track
═══════	hiking route on a street
▬ ▬ ▬ ▬	hiking route on a path
••••••••	hiking route without a path
....ALT....	alternative route, short-cut
ST	street
FW	dirt road, sandy track
– MP – –	monopáti, mule track
←⇐	walking direction/alternative
– – – – –	dry streambed (at times), hollow
⚕	antenna
Ⓑ ⒝	bus stop / - seasonal
Ⓟ	parking area
Ⓣ	petrol station
Ⓗ	helicopter landing pad
▦	cemetery
+	wayside shrine, monument
◯	sports field
⌒	cave
♪ ♂	medieval castle, dwelling tower / ruins
⚒	ancient ruins, statue
▪ ▫	houses/ruins
♠ ♠	monastery, large church/ruins
♦ ♦ ♦	chapel/summit chapel/ruins
▼ ▽	taverna/ - open seasonally
✳	windmill, ruins
◘ ▫▫	fountain, well, spring, reservoir, cistern
S	swimming possible

In the text:

!!	pay attention to turn-off!
↙	possible feelings of vertigo
OW	time for walking one way
★	the author's 18 favourite spots